W9-BFA-468

Cooking with HAWAIIAN MAGIC

At Last!
Island Recipes and Luau Ideas
for our Mainland Friends

by
Mae and Lee Keao

Original Illustrations
by
Missy Blalack

BESS PRESS, INC.
P.O. Box 22388
Honolulu, Hawaii 96822

In Memory Of My Late And Beloved Mother
Abigail T. Keao
Who Taught Me The Skills Of The Kitchen As
My Dad Taught Me The Ways Of The Ocean
Lee

For My Wonderful Mother
Mamie Edwards
A Gracious Hostess And Talented Cook
Mae

Keao's Hawaiian Enterprises, Inc. has no reason to doubt that recipe ingredients, instructions, and directions will work successfully. However, the ingredients, instructions and directions have not necessarily been thoroughly or systematically tested, and the cook should not hesitate to test and question procedures and directions before preparation. The recipes in this book have been collected from various sources, and neither Keao's Hawaiian Enterprises, Inc. nor any contributor, publisher, printer, distributor or seller of this book is responsible for errors or omissions.

Copyright © 1990 by The Bess Press, Inc.

ALL RIGHTS RESERVED

Printed in the United States of America

LIBRARY OF CONGRESS CATALOG CARD NUMBER: 89-81703

Keao, Mae and Lee
    Cooking with Hawaiian Magic
Honolulu, Hawaii: Bess Press, Inc.
    160 pages

REVISED EDITION

ISBN: 0-935848-77-0

Hawaiian Magic

Aloha Friends,

Hawaii is a blend of cultures from all over the world. Each new group of immigrants to the Islands has brought its own special customs, foods, and cooking methods - Chinese, Japanese, Korean, Portuguese, Filipino, and even the "Haole" (Mainlanders). As a result, Hawaiian cuisine blends these traditions into something truly unique and delicious.

We have written this cookbook to share the magic of Hawaii that we have experienced in our lives. We have drawn from our personal knowledge to share our love of the Islands with our Mainland friends. In many instances, these are traditional recipes which have been passed from generation to generation.

We want this book to be fun and easy to use. **Hawaiian Magic** can be used for all occasions, not just special events. Many Hawaiian dishes are simple to make and great for anyone's everyday use. For example, our stir-fry dishes are "wiki wiki" (quick) - perfect for busy families! We have also included a special section on how to give a Luau, so you can create your own enchanted tropical evening.

Our desire, in writing this book, has been to share our love of Hawaii so you can experience its magic, too.

Mahalo Nui Loa,
Mae and Lee

Many Mahalos to those who contributed their cherished recipes, time, enthusiasm and support to this book.

Editor in Chief:
Nancy Maynard

Editors:
Sandy Plaisance
Lesleigh Dodd
Revē Shapard
Ann Rayson
David Keao, Jr.
Becky Keao
Paula Keao
Laverna Shirai
Lehua Kahiapo
Jan Cook
Judy Rowell
Dole Foods
Mauna Loa Macadamia Nut Corporation
Small Business Development Center at University of South Alabama
Hawaiian Visitors Bureau

Contents

MAGICAL MENUS

Polynesian Prince *(Dinner)*

Diamondhead Prime Rib Roast

Lobster Tail Lahaina - Fluffy Gourmet Rice

Spinach Salad Lehua

Haupia Cake

Iced Tea - Coffee Smoothie

Bora Bora *(Rehearsal Dinner)*

Spare Ribs Pacifica

Sunset Salad - Fluffy Hot Rice

Ice Cream da Pineapple Way

Haupia

Sunset Spritz

Hot Coffee

Tiki Tiki Waikiki *(Dinner)*

Spicy Orange Chicken - Chinese Peas

Secret Shrimp Fried Rice

Coconut Puffs

Coffee

Wicked Wahini *(Wild Woman)* Luncheon

Hot and Sour Soup

Island Lemon Chicken - Pineapple Rubies

Light Beverage

Honeymooners' Delight *(Breakfast)*

Sunrise Omelet

Banana Spice Coffee Cake
(with cream cheese)

Frozen Heaven

Hot Coffee

Pupu Party *(Appetizers)*

Teriyaki Kabob Pupus · Sesame Sherry Sticks

Miniature Drumsticks

Crisp Won Tons

High Voltage Mustard Sauce

Sweet and Sour Sauce

Hawaiian Coconut Nog

Bridal Tea

Hawaiian Wedding Cake · Miniature Quiche

Sesame Sherry Sticks

Paradise Punch

Starry Starry Night *(Dinner For Two)*

Hot Spinach Salad

Bird of Paradise

Fresh Pineapple Mist

Coconut Mousse

Hot Coffee

Mainland Luau

Volcano Watermelon

Honey of a Honeydew

Sweet and Sour Chicken Wings

Smart and Sassy Shrimp

Chicken with Long Rice

Hawaiian Short Ribs

Haupia

Orange Bread

Banana Nut Bread

Tahitian Ice Cream Cake

Beverage of Your Choice

Tropical Heat Wave *(Teenagers' Delight)*

Puka Burgers

Pineapple Outriggers - Surf Baked Beans

Chinese Almond Cookies

Sunset Spritz

Keiki *(Little One)* Only

Macadamia Nut Ice Cream Dessert

Ginger Dreams

Rainbow Sparklers

A Note On Recipes

We hope you enjoy making and serving all the recipes in HAWAIIAN MAGIC as much as we have enjoyed gathering and testing them. Your results will be better if you keep the following points in mind:

— We recommend vegetable oil or vegetable shortening in recipes, as it has a lighter taste and is better for you than animal fats. Vegetable oil may also be called salad oil or cooking oil. Peanut oil gives especially good results in stir-fry recipes because of its delicious taste and its ability to be heated to high temperatures. Sesame oil should not be substituted for other oils because it breaks down when heated. Sesame oil is primarily an Oriental flavoring.

— When flour is listed as an ingredient in a recipe, we mean all-purpose flour. Special flours such as self-rising or wheat are indicated, specifically when necessary for best results.

— Always firmly pack brown sugar into a measuring cup to obtain the correct amount.

— Foods that may be unfamiliar to Mainlanders have been marked with an asterisk. A Glossary appears at the end of HAWAIIAN MAGIC to familiarize you with these ingredients. We have also suggested possible sources for finding these foods, as well as substitutes.

Pupus

"Pupus", Hawaiian finger foods, snacks, or appetizers, are served generously in the Islands. Their exotic flavors are extracted from local favorites. Macadamia nuts, small bits of meats, vegetables and Oriental specialties. . .they are usually served with a zesty sauce.

Add a bowl of rice and you have a meal or a menu for a "Pupu" party.

Teriyaki Kabob Pupus

1 pound	sirloin steak or rib-eye steak
½ cup	pineapple syrup (from can of pineapple)
¼ cup	soy sauce
1 tablespoon	sugar
1 teaspoon	peeled ginger root*, grated
1 clove	garlic, grated
1 (8 ounce) can	pineapple chunks
16	whole water chestnuts*
16	stuffed green olives

Cut meat into 16 cubes, ¾ inch thick. Mix pineapple syrup, soy sauce, sugar, ginger root and garlic. Marinate meat for 1 hour in this mixture, turning occasionally. Using half of a barbecue stick, thread a cube of meat, pineapple chunks, and a water chestnut on each stick. Broil 3 inches from heat for 5 minutes. Turn and broil other side for 5 minutes. Garnish end of each stick with a stuffed olive. Serve piping hot.
Makes 16 kabobs.

Lomi Lomi Salmon*

1 pound	salted salmon
5	large ripe tomatoes, peeled
1	medium onion, chopped fine
1 bunch	green onions, thinly sliced, including tops
	crushed ice

Soak salmon in cold water for 3 hours. Remove the salmon from the water and remove skin and bones. Using a fork, shred salmon to a fine texture. Place tomatoes in a large bowl and mash with a fork or squeeze to a pulp. Add the salmon, onion and green onions to the tomato mixture and mix until well blended. Chill. Just before serving add crushed ice.

This will become watery from the crushed ice, so when ready to store, drain some of the liquid out. Leave some of the liquid in to keep moist, cover and refrigerate. This is delicious as a side dish and goes very well with cone sushi or as a light snack with saltine crackers. *Serves 8.*

Sweet and Sour Meatballs

½ cup	milk
½ pound	ground beef
½ cup	soft bread
¼ teaspoon	salt
	chopped onions
1 tablespoon	vinegar
2 tablespoons	sugar
1 tablespoon	Worcestershire sauce
½ cup	ketchup

Mix bread, meat, milk, salt, and onions well and form into balls. Fry in fat until browned. Combine vinegar, sugar, Worcestershire and ketchup. Pour sauce over meatballs and simmer for ½ hour. Just before serving, spear each ball with a pretzel.
Serves 4.

Pupu Drumettes

12	chicken wing drumettes
2 tablespoons	Sake*
1 teaspoon	salt
	dash of black pepper
¼ cup	cornstarch
3 tablespoons	sugar
½ cup	soy sauce
2 teaspoons	peeled, minced ginger root*
2 cloves	garlic, mashed
2 teaspoons	sesame seeds, crushed
	chili pepper (optional)
1 cup	flour
	oil for frying

Combine chicken, Sake, salt, pepper and cornstarch; mix well and set aside. In a saucepan, combine sugar, soy sauce, ginger, garlic and sesame seeds and bring to a boil. Flour chicken and fry until golden brown. Immediately dip into soy sauce mixture. Serve warm.
Makes 12 appetizers.

Chicken Wings With Oyster Sauce (Ho Yow Gai Yick)

If desired, you can substitute chicken legs, though this is not what the Chinese use. This is a good hot appetizer, or serve with rice for a main dish.

8	chicken wings
1 large clove	garlic
⅓ cup	water
4 tablespoons	oyster sauce*
1 tablespoon	soy sauce (or less)
1 teaspoon	sugar
1 tablespoon	oil
6 thin slices	peeled ginger root*

Cut chicken wings into 3 pieces each and cut off wing tips. Smash garlic clove and peel. Mix water, oyster sauce, soy sauce and sugar. In a deep heavy skillet or wok, heat oil until medium hot. Add ginger root and garlic; stir-fry until brown, then discard. Add oyster sauce mixture and chicken wings and bring to a boil. Reduce heat, cover, and simmer for 30 minutes. Every 10 minutes turn wings and check liquid. If liquid gets too low, add hot water. Remove cover, increase heat to medium, cook and stir until all surfaces are covered with sauce and no sauce remains in pan.
Serves 4.

Sesame Sherry Sticks

1 (10 ounce) package	pie crust mix
1 cup	grated cheese
½ cup	sherry
¼ cup	sesame seeds
½ teaspoon	garlic salt

Lightly grease baking sheets. Make pie crust mix according to package directions, adding cheese when mixing crust. Use sherry for liquid instead of water. Shape dough into small sticks, using about 1 teaspoonful of dough for each. Roll sticks in sesame seeds and place about 1 inch apart on prepared baking sheets. Bake at 425 degrees about 8 to 10 minutes. Serve hot or cold. Store cooled sticks in air tight containers.
Makes 3 dozen appetizers.

Miniature Drumsticks

20	chicken wings (about 3 pounds)
2 tablespoons	salad oil
½ cup	soy sauce
⅓ cup	medium or dry sherry
¼ cup	ketchup
2 tablespoons	sugar
¼ teaspoon	peeled, ground ginger root*
	lettuce, shredded

A day ahead or about 1 hour before serving, cut wing tips off at joint. Cut each wing in half at joint. In 5 quart Dutch oven or sauce pot, heat salad oil and fry chicken wings, stirring constantly, about 7 minutes. Reduce heat to medium, add remaining ingredients except shredded lettuce, stirring to blend well. Cover and cook about 25 minutes, stirring occasionally. Uncover Dutch oven and cook 10 minutes longer, stirring frequently, until almost all liquid is absorbed. Cover and refrigerate to serve cold on bed of shredded lettuce or serve warm.
Makes 40 appetizers.

Crisp Won Ton

A very simple illustration on how to fold a won ton is shown on package wrappers of raw won ton pi. Won ton pi are usually found in the specialty cooler section at your store or the Oriental food store.

½ pound	pork, chopped fine
¼ teaspoon	sugar
½ teaspoon	soy sauce
2 drops	sesame oil*
½ teaspoon	salt
1 stalk	green onion, chopped fine
8	shrimp, chopped
2	water chestnuts*, chopped
	pepper
1 pound	won ton pi*

Mix all ingredients except won ton pi. Place ½ teaspoon filling in the center of a piece of won ton pi. Fold in half diagonally, forming a triangle. Moisten edge and seal by pressing firmly together. Turn pointed top of triangle to meet the fold. Turn folded side down. Overlap opposite corners, moisten and press together. Deep fry until brown and crisp. Drain on paper towels.
Makes 18 to 24 won tons.

Tahitian Raw Fish

1 pound	fresh raw fish
1 teaspoon	coarse salt
	juice of 6 limes
2 tablespoons	chopped green onion
1 clove	garlic
1 cup	coconut milk

Cut fish into bite sized pieces. Sprinkle with salt and cover with lime juice. Cover and refrigerate at least four hours. Drain off the lime juice. Add the rest of the ingredients. Chill until time to serve. Arrange on a bed of lettuce.
Serves 4-6.

Crab Won Tons

1 (8 ounce) package	cream cheese, softened
1 (8 ounce) package	frozen crabmeat, thawed and drained
36	won ton pi*
	peanut oil

Mix together cream cheese and crabmeat in bowl. Place 1 teaspoon in middle of won ton pi; moisten edges with cold water; fold over meat mixture and form a triangle; seal edges by pressing together. Prepare remaining won tons in the same manner. Heat two or three inches of oil in skillet or wok until hot. Fry 2 or 3 won tons at a time until golden brown. Drain on paper towels. You may keep won tons hot while frying by placing them on a heat proof dish in a 250 degree oven. Serve with Sweet and Sour Sauce (see Index).
Makes 36 pieces.

Sweet and Sour Chicken Wings

2 pounds	chicken wings
	garlic powder
	salt
	pepper
2	eggs, beaten
	cornstarch
	vegetable oil
1 tablespoon	soy sauce
3 tablespoons	ketchup
½ cup	sugar
¼ cup	vinegar
¾ cup	chicken stock

Cut tips off wings. Cut wings in half at joint. Season chicken with garlic powder, salt, and pepper. Dip chicken wings in egg. Roll in cornstarch. Fry to brown in oil. Arrange in pan lined with foil. Combine soy sauce, ketchup, sugar, vinegar, and chicken stock. Pour sauce over chicken. Bake at 350 degrees for 45 minutes to 1 hour. Turn every 15 minutes.
Serves 6.

Lomi Lomi Salmon Spread

1 (8 ounce) package	cream cheese, softened
1 (3 ounce) package	smoked salmon, cubed
1 teaspoon	lemon juice
1 tablespoon	chopped onion
1 tablespoon	thinly sliced green onions

Combine cream cheese, salmon, lemon juice and onion; mix until well blended. Sprinkle with green onions. Serve with crisp crackers or melba toast.
Serves 6-8.

Miniature Quiche

½ cup	grated Swiss cheese
½ cup	butter
1 cup	flour
2	eggs, beaten
⅓ cup	milk
2 tablespoons	bacon or ham, chopped
1 teaspoon	chopped green onion
2 tablespoons	sliced mushrooms
	salt and pepper to taste
½ cup	cooked spinach

Combine cheese, butter and flour. Mix into a smooth dough and chill in refrigerator for 30 minutes. In separate bowl, combine eggs, milk, bacon or ham, green onion, mushrooms, and salt and pepper; set aside. Form dough mixture into 1-inch balls and press into compartments of a miniature muffin pan. Place cooked spinach at the bottom of each compartment and gradually pour in custard filling. Bake at 400 degrees in oven until firm, about 5 to 15 minutes. Cool before removing from pan.
Serves 6-8.

Sunset Spritz

This is a wonderfully refreshing and pretty beverage you may want to prepare ahead by keeping fruit cubes frozen and stored in freezer.

	fresh fruit; your choice of lemon, lime, cherries, strawberries, or pineapple chunks or a combination. Bottled cherries are nice too.
1 (2 liter) bottle	clear lemon-lime carbonated beverage or ginger ale

Slice fruit into bite sized pieces. Place one piece of fruit into each cubicle of an ice tray. Fill with water and freeze until set. To serve, fill tall clear glasses with 6 or 8 fruit ice cubes and pour in clear beverage. Garnish with fresh pineapple slice, lemon or lime wedge or miniature umbrella.

Yields approximately 2 quarts.

Coffee Smoothie

You may use any excellent quality coffee with this.

2 cups	strong Kona coffee*, cold
2 bananas	(optional)
1 pint	coffee ice cream, softened

Blend coffee, bananas, and ice cream thoroughly in blender for 30 seconds, or until smooth.

Serves 4.

Kona Coffee

The Big Island of Hawaii boasts the only commercial coffee plantation in the United States. Here homegrown and roasted coffee beans are produced. Thus, the birth of the much sought after gourmet-status Kona coffee.

You can find it in gourmet shops, or special delicatessens.

Rainbow Sparklers

Especially for Beau and Lauren.

3 quarts	**water, divided (1 quart per envelope of soft drink mix)**
1 (1 ounce) package	**of each of the following powdered artificially sweetened soft drink mixes: grape, lime, and cherry**
1 (2 liter) bottle	**clear lemon-lime carbonated beverage, chilled**

Using a large pitcher, pour in 1 quart water; add grape powder and stir. Fill divided ice trays with all of liquid. Freeze. Repeat process for lime and cherry soft drink powders. You will have purple, green and red ice cubes.

To serve, fill clear plastic cups with an ice cube of each color. Pour clear carbonated beverage over ice cubes. Add a colorful straw.

Children love to join in to "help" make this drink. When the cubes begin to melt, the drink looks like a rainbow.
Yields 1½ gallons.

Fresh Pineapple Mist

1	fresh whole pineapple
¾ cup	ginger ale, chilled
¼ cup	orange juice, chilled
1 tablespoon	lime juice

Remove green top from pineapple and rinse pineapple thoroughly. Cut pineapple into quarters. Remove fruit from shell, core and cut into large chunks. Whip about 4 chunks at a time in a blender at high speed until puréed. Add all the puréed pineapple chunks back into the blender jar along with the ginger ale, orange juice, and lime juice. Whip on low speed until blended. Pour into tall glasses and garnish with decorated straws and fresh mint leaves.
Serves 4.

NOTE: This recipe can also be served in a whole pineapple by removing about ¼-inch off the top. Using a knife or spoon, gently scoop out pineapple meat, leaving whole shell intact. Follow instructions on how to purée and add rest of ingredients until blended. Chill until ready to serve. Pour pineapple mixture into the pineapple shell and serve with 2 thin decorated straws and garnish with a fresh mint leaf.

Tropical Tea

4 cups	boiling water
4	tea bags
½ cup	sugar
8	limes
4 cups	unsweetened pineapple juice, chilled
2 (28 ounce) bottles	ginger ale, chilled
	fresh strawberries

Pour boiling water over tea bags in a 1-gallon container. Let stand 3 to 5 minutes, remove tea bags and stir in sugar. Cut limes in half and squeeze out the juice to make 1 cup. Put the lime juice and lime rinds aside. Stir the chilled pineapple juice into the tea mixture. This can be prepared ahead of time. Just before serving, add lime juice and ginger ale, and stir until well blended. Serve over ice cubes or pour over frozen ice ring. Place a strawberry in center of each lime rind to garnish and float on top of tea punch.

If preferred, make ice ring by making an extra batch of tea mixture but omitting the lime juice. Add sliced strawberries to ring before serving.

Serves 12.

Paradise Punch

¾ tablespoon	peeled ginger root*, finely chopped
1¾ cups	sugar
7 cups	water
1½ cups	guava* juice
2¼ cups	fresh pineapple juice
2½ cups	orange juice (1 dozen small oranges)
½ cup	lemon juice (4 small lemons)
2 tablespoons	fresh mint leaves, finely chopped

Boil chopped ginger with 3 cups of water until a strong ginger flavor is obtained. Cool and strain through cloth, squeezing ginger root. Boil sugar and remaining 4 cups of water to make syrup, then cool. Combine all ingredients and pour over cracked ice. If punch is too strong, dilute with water.

Yields 12 cups.

Pineapple Cooler

4 cups	unsweetened pineapple juice, chilled
½ cup	lemon juice
1 (2 liter) bottle	lemon-lime carbonated beverage
	canned or fresh pineapple slices

Combine fruit juices in a 3 quart container; mix well. This can be prepared ahead of time. Just before serving, add the lemon-lime beverage. Serve over ice cubes or pour over ice ring in punch bowl. Garnish with pineapple slices.
Yields 2½ quarts.

Hawaiian Coconut Nog

1 (8½ ounce) can	cream of coconut
1 (13 ounce) can	evaporated milk
1 cup	cola
½ teaspoon	vanilla flavoring
1 cup	sugar
4	eggs
	Maraschino cherries, optional

Combine the cream of coconut, evaporated milk, cola, vanilla, sugar and eggs in a blender container and blend until smooth. Chill until ready to serve. Garnish each serving with one cherry.
Yields 1 quart.

Jade East Tofu Soup

2 tablespoons	peanut oil
1½ cups	sliced fresh mushrooms
3 large cloves	garlic, peeled and crushed
½ teaspoon	peeled and minced fresh ginger root*
3 tablespoons	soy sauce
2½ cups	chicken stock
1½ cups	water
1 cup	uncooked egg noodles
1	unpeeled medium zucchini, cut in ½-inch pieces
1 cup	cleaned and finely chopped fresh spinach
¼ pound	tofu*, cut in ½-inch cubes
⅓ cup	finely chopped green onions, including tops

Heat oil in wok over high heat. Add next 3 ingredients; stir-fry 2 minutes. Add soy sauce; take off heat. Bring stock and water to boil in another Dutch oven over high heat; add noodles; boil 2 minutes; reduce heat to simmer; add zucchini and spinach; simmer 6 to 8 minutes. Add tofu and reserved mushroom mixture; simmer 8 to 10 minutes. Garnish with green onions. Serve immediately.
Serves 4-6.

Hot And Sour Soup

¼ pound	pork fillet
6	cloud ear mushrooms*
¼ cup	bok choy*
2 cakes	tofu*
15	lily buds*
1 tablespoon	soy sauce
1 teaspoon	sugar
1 teaspoon	white pepper
2 tablespoons	white vinegar
2 tablespoons	cornstarch
¼ cup	water
1	egg
2	scallions
4 cups	chicken broth
2 teaspoons	sesame oil*

Cut pork fillet into ⅛ inch slices and then into very narrow strips 1½ to 2 inches long. Wash cloud ear mushrooms and soak in warm water for 30 minutes. Wash again, dry, and shred. Shred bok choy. Slice cakes of tofu in half to make 2 thin squares and then shred. Wash the lily buds and soak 30 minutes in warm water; remove hard ends and cut each into 3 pieces. In a cup, mix vinegar, soy sauce, sugar, and pepper. In a separate cup, mix cornstarch and water. Beat egg until frothy. Mince the scallions. In a soup pan, mix chicken broth, cloud ear mushrooms, lily buds, and bok choy. Boil over medium heat for 8 minutes. Add pork; mix and cook for 1 minute. Add shredded tofu and the soy sauce mixture; mix and cook ½ minute. Add cornstarch mixture and cook and stir for 1 minute. Remove from heat and add the beaten egg very slowly, drop by drop. Mix in the sesame oil and scallions.
Serves 4.

Nancy Maynard

Watercress Soup

If you are fortunate enough to have fresh watercress available, try this one. Sooo good!

8 cups	chicken stock
½ teaspoon	Five Spices*
2 teaspoons	salt
1 teaspoon	sugar
2 tablespoons	dry sherry
2	¼-inch slices fresh ginger root*, peeled
4	green onions, sliced
2 bunches	watercress, washed, stems discarded
½ cup	thinly sliced ham

Put first 7 ingredients in Dutch oven over high heat; bring to boil; cook 10 minutes; strain, reserving stock. Return stock to Dutch oven over high heat; bring to boil; add watercress and ham; return to boil. Serve immediately.
Serves 6-8.

Chinese Rice Soup (Chuk)

	left over turkey bones
6 quarts	water
1 head	bok choy*
2 cups	rice, washed and drained
2 stalks	celery, cut in halves
1 (13¾ ounce) can	clear chicken broth
2½ teaspoons	salt
1 teaspoon	monosodium glutamate
2 stalks	green onion, chopped
¼ cup	shredded lettuce

In a large pot, add turkey bones, bok choy, celery, and water. Cook for 1 hour. Remove bones, bok choy, and celery. Debone meat. Strain stock and return to pot. Add rice, salt, meat, and cook for 1½ hours. Add broth and cook for another ½ hour. Add green onion, monosodium glutamate, and stir. Turn heat off. Serve garnished with lettuce.
Serves 8-10.

Egg Flower Soup

1 quart	chicken broth
½ cup	water chestnuts*, finely chopped
2	eggs, beaten
¼ teaspoon	pepper

Pour chicken broth in a large pot or soup kettle. Cover and cook over medium heat until it reaches the boiling point. Continue to boil for about 6 minutes. Add chopped water chestnuts to the boiling broth and cook for 5 minutes. Add beaten eggs slowly and stir until eggs form "small flowers". This occurs immediately. Season with pepper and reduce heat.

Serves 4.

Egg Drop Soup With Shrimp

6 cups	chicken stock
	salt and freshly ground
	white pepper to taste
	pinch cayenne pepper
½ cup	frozen petite green peas
16	medium shrimp, shelled
	and deveined
2 tablespoons	cornstarch mixed with
	¼ cup cold water
2	eggs, lightly beaten with
	1 teaspoon soy sauce
2	green onions, thinly
	sliced

Heat chicken stock, salt, pepper and cayenne pepper in saucepan over high heat to just under a boil. Add peas; cook 1 minute. Add shrimp; cook until pink. Add cornstarch mixture, stirring until slightly thickened. Remove from heat; beat in eggs. Garnish with onions; serve immediately.

Serves 6-8.

Layered Salad, Lahaina

During our visit to the Islands this summer, we were eating at a neat little restaurant on the North Shore of Oahu. We were eating an outlandishly delicious green salad, when it dawned on me that nearly every restaurant we had eaten in had served salads either layered or "arranged"—not tossed. To me, this enhanced the fresh flavors of the vegetables and fruits. Out of curiosity, I tried to find the word salad in the Hawaiian language and there wasn't a word for it. Very interesting.

Mae

1 head	lettuce, finely chopped
2 cups	celery, thinly sliced
½ cup	green onions, thinly sliced
2 (8 ounce) cans	water chestnuts*, drained and sliced
1 (20 ounce) package	frozen green petite peas, uncooked
1½ cups	mayonnaise
1 teaspoon	seasoned salt
1 tablespoon	sugar
	garlic powder, according to taste
½ cup	Parmesan cheese (may use more if desired)
1 pound	crisp bacon, crumbled
3-4	hard cooked eggs, as garnish

Layer first 6 ingredients in the order given. Over the mayonnaise layer, sprinkle seasoned salt, sugar, garlic powder and Parmesan cheese. Cover and chill well (better overnight). Before serving, add bacon and garnish with eggs.
Serves 10-12.

Maui Fruit Salad

This is a great party pleaser. The combination of these ingredients has such a surprising taste and makes a beautiful entrance when artistically arranged on a pretty platter.

2	large ripe papayas*, peeled and sliced
2	ripe avocadoes, peeled and sliced
6	ripe tomatoes, peeled and sliced
1	small purple onion, sliced into thin rings
	Boston or Manoa lettuce
2 teaspoons	salt
1 teaspoon	white pepper
½ teaspoon	cracked black pepper
¼ teaspoon	sugar
½ teaspoon	dry mustard
	juice of ½ lemon
1 clove	garlic, pressed
5 tablespoons	tarragon vinegar
½ cup	vegetable oil
2 tablespoons	olive oil
1	coddled egg (boil for one minute), lightly beaten
½ cup	light cream

Prepare the fruit and vegetables and arrange in sections on a lettuce lined platter. Combine remaining ingredients in a jar with a tightly fitting lid. Shake vigorously. Pour over sliced fruit and vegetables when ready to serve.
Serves 6-8.

Hula Ula Ula Salad

1 (6 ounce) package	strawberry gelatin
1 cup	boiling water
3	bananas, sliced
2 (10 ounce) packages	frozen, sliced strawberries, not drained
2 cups	walnuts, coarsely chopped
1 (20 ounce) can	crushed pineapple, not drained
1 pint	sour cream

Dissolve strawberry gelatin in 1 cup boiling water. Mix bananas, strawberries, nuts, and crushed pineapple together and add to gelatin. Pour half of mixture in a flat pan and let set in refrigerator until firm, then spread sour cream over layer. Spoon remaining mixture over sour cream and let set until firm.
Serves 6-8.

Melon Balls In Port

Fill sherbet glasses with balls of watermelon, honeydew and cantaloupe. Pour two tablespoons port wine over each glass of fruit. Chill well before serving.

Spinach Salad, Lehua

This salad's flavors are greatly enhanced if prepared the night before. It is very picturesque served in a large clear glass bowl. Make this and take a bow.

2 bunches	**spinach, washed, trimmed and torn in bite sized pieces**
1 teaspoon	**sugar**
6	**hard cooked eggs, chopped**
½ pound	**ham, julienned**
1 (10 ounce) box	**frozen petite peas, half thawed**
1	**flat round white onion, thinly sliced and separated in rings**
1 cup	**sour cream**
1 cup	**mayonnaise**
½ pound	**Swiss cheese, grated**
1 pound	**bacon, fried, drained and crumbled**

On the bottom of a 4-quart shallow glass serving bowl, place ½ of the spinach. Sprinkle with ½ teaspoon sugar. Next place the eggs and ham, then another layer of spinach and ½ teaspoon sugar. Add the peas and the onion. Mix the sour cream and mayonnaise and spread evenly to the edge of the salad to seal. Cover and refrigerate overnight. When ready to serve, top with the grated Swiss cheese and crumbled bacon.
Serves 8-10.

Fresh Lemony Fruit And Vegetable Bowl

½	large Dole® fresh pineapple
⅓ cup	fresh lemon juice
1 tablespoon	white wine vinegar
2 tablespoons	sugar
¾ teaspoon	oregano, crumbled
¾ teaspoon	thyme, crumbled
¼ teaspoon	salt
¾ cup	vegetable oil
1 tablespoon	freshly grated lemon peel
½ pound	broccoli, cut in flowerettes
3	medium carrots, peeled and sliced ¼ inch thick
1 small head	cauliflower, cut in flowerettes

Remove pineapple from shell; core and cut fruit into chunks. Place in large shallow casserole dish. For dressing, combine lemon juice, vinegar, sugar, herbs and salt in blender. Slowly pour in oil, whir until mixture is well blended. Stir in lemon peel. Pour dressing over pineapple. Cook broccoli, carrots and cauliflower until tender-crisp. Toss warm vegetables with dressing and pineapple. Chill overnight. Serve at room temperature.
Serves 6-8.

Orchid Chicken Salad

1 (15¼ ounce) can	pineapple tidbits, undrained
4 cups	chopped cooked chicken
1 (11 ounce) can	mandarin oranges, drained
1 (8 ounce) can	sliced water chestnuts*, drained
1 (2½ ounce) package	sliced almonds, toasted
1 cup	chopped celery
1 cup	seedless white grapes, sliced in half
1½ cups	mayonnaise
1 tablespoon	soy sauce
1 teaspoon	curry powder
1 (3 ounce) can	chow mein noodles lettuce leaves

Drain pineapple, reserving 2 tablespoons juice. Combine pineapple, chicken, oranges, water chestnuts, almonds, celery and grapes; mix well.

Combine the 2 tablespoons pineapple juice, mayonnaise, soy sauce and curry powder; stir well and add to chicken mixture. Chill. Stir in chow mein noodles just before serving. Serve salad on lettuce leaves. *Serves 8.*

Curried Chicken Salad In Tomato Petals

---

2 cups	cooked chicken, diced
1	apple, pared and diced
½ cup	celery, diced
2 teaspoons	onion, grated
½ cup	seedless grapes, halved
⅓ cup	almonds, toasted and slivered
2 teaspoons	curry powder
1 cup	mayonnaise
1 teaspoon	salt
	dash of pepper
6	tomatoes
	parsley sprigs

Combine chicken, apple, celery, onion, grapes, and almonds. Blend curry powder with mayonnaise and seasonings; stir into chicken mixture. Chill. Cut tomatoes in sixths, almost but not all the way through, to form petals. Fill tomatoes with chicken salad. Garnish with parsley sprigs. For contrast, serve on a bed of deep green fresh spinach. *Serves 6.*

Tropical Crab Or Shrimp Salad

2½ cups	diced fresh pineapple
1½ cups	shredded crabmeat or boiled baby shrimp
¾ cup	mayonnaise
1½ tablespoons	ketchup
1 teaspoon	Worcestershire sauce

Serve the pineapple and crab or shrimp on crisp lettuce leaves. Add the ketchup and Worcestershire sauce to the mayonnaise and serve over the salad. If desired, add a teaspoon of sweet pickle relish and ½ teaspoon finely minced onion to mayonnaise.
Serves 6.

Baked Crab Salad

2 (8 ounce) cans	crabmeat
¾ cup	mayonnaise
2 tablespoons	lemon juice
¼ teaspoon	salt
¼ teaspoon	garlic salt
½ teaspoon	chili powder
2 teaspoons	Worcestershire sauce
½ cup	celery, finely diced
2	medium tomatoes, diced (1¼ cups)
¼ cup	green onion, minced
2 cups	corn chips

Drain and flake crab. In a mixing bowl, thoroughly mix together mayonnaise, lemon juice, salt, garlic salt, chili powder, and Worcestershire sauce. Mix in the crab, celery, tomatoes, and green onion. In the bottom of a buttered shallow 1-quart baking dish, place a layer of corn chips. Top with crab mixture. Top with remaining corn chips. Bake at 350 degrees for 15 to 20 minutes, and serve at once.
Serves 4-6.

Chinese Vegetable Salad

8 sheets	won ton pi*
1 medium head	Romaine or Manoa lettuce
1 small head	iceberg lettuce
¼ cup	Chinese parsley*, chopped
1 tablespoon	sesame seeds, toasted lightly
½ cup	green onion, chopped
15	water chestnuts*, thinly sliced

Cut won ton pi into triangles or strips. Deep fry in oil until brown. Place on absorbent paper. Wash vegetables; drain thoroughly. Tear or shred greens into bite sized pieces. Add parsley, green onion, and water chestnuts to greens. Chill well. Before serving, add sesame seeds, won ton pi, and toss lightly with Chinese Sesame Dressing (see Index).
Serves 4-6.

Tropical Fruit Platter

1	medium fresh pineapple
1	medium papaya*
2	medium bananas, sliced
2 cups	pink or white grapefruit sections
2 cups	melon balls
2 cups	avocado, sliced
	lime twist and mint for decoration

Twist crown from pineapple. Peel, quarter pineapple lengthwise and cut off core. Cut fruit into spears. Pare, halve and seed papaya. Cut fruit into spears. Peel, seed and cut avocado. Arrange all fruits on chilled platter. Decorate with lime and mint, and serve with Ginger Lime Dressing. (See Index).
Serves 8.

Manoa Salad

Manoa is a type of Hawaiian lettuce, but Mainlanders can substitute iceberg or other varieties of lettuce.

> 1 cup   celery, cut into thin
> slants
> 1 head   lettuce, broken into bite
> sized pieces
> 1 cup   green onion, finely
> chopped
> 3½ cups   cabbage, shredded
> 1   small cucumber, cut
> into ¼-inch slices

Combine ingredients. Toss with Chinese Sesame Dressing (See Index) just before serving.
Serves 4-6.

Hot Spinach Salad

½ pound	bacon, chopped
2 bunches	fresh spinach, rinsed well
¼ pound	fresh mushrooms, thinly sliced
2	hard-cooked eggs, grated
½ cup	grated Parmesan cheese
	freshly ground black pepper
2 tablespoons	olive oil
3 tablespoons	red wine vinegar
	juice of ½ lemon
½ tablespoon	Worcestershire sauce

Fry bacon until crisp. Drain on absorbent paper; reserve drippings. In a large clear glass bowl combine the spinach leaves, mushrooms, eggs, bacon, Parmesan cheese and pepper; toss lightly to mix. Warm reserved bacon drippings, olive oil, red wine vinegar, lemon juice and Worcestershire sauce over medium-high heat. Pour the dressing over hot spinach mixture; toss lightly and serve at once. Sprinkle with additional pepper, if desired.
Serves 2-4.

Sunset Salad

1 cup	seedless grapes
1 cup	cubed pineapple
1 cup	fresh or frozen coconut, thawed
1 cup	mandarin oranges
1 cup	seeded lychees*, canned
1 cup	minature marshmallows
1 cup	sour cream

Combine and chill overnight.
Serves 8.

Plantation Chicken Salad

3 cups	cooked white meat of chicken
½ cup	orange juice
⅔ cup	finely diced celery
1 (3½ ounce) jar	Bits O' Macadamia Nuts®*
1½ teaspoons	salt
½ cup	mayonnaise
2	large oranges, sectioned
	lettuce leaves

Marinate chicken in orange juice for 20 minutes. Drain. Combine chicken, celery, macadamia nuts, salt, mayonnaise and orange sections; mix gently. Serve on lettuce leaves. Garnish with cherry tomatoes and more macadamia nuts, if desired.
Serves 6.

Curried Ham Salad

6 ounces	cream cheese, softened
¼ cup	creamy peanut butter
¼ cup	minced green onion
¼ cup	pineapple juice
1 tablespoon	cider vinegar
1 tablespoon	honey
2 teaspoons	prepared mustard
1 teaspoon	curry powder
1½ pounds	ham, cut into ½ inch cubes
3 tablespoons	raisins
3	large green bell peppers
6	lettuce leaves
12	wedges fresh pineapple
½ cup	chopped salted roasted peanuts

In a large bowl, combine cream cheese, peanut butter, green onion, pineapple juice, vinegar, honey, mustard and curry. Stir vigorously to blend well. Fold in ham and raisins. Cut green peppers horizontally in half. Remove seeds and membrane; trim stem. Fill each pepper half with ham salad. Arrange on serving plates lined with lettuce. Garnish each with two pineapple wedges. Sprinkle peanuts over salads before serving.
Serves 6.

Steamed Bass Hawaiian Style

This is a super way to complement the catch of the day. I first ate steamed fish served this way at a family Luau. I forgot the rest of the food!

Mae

1	sea bass or striped bass (about 3 pounds cleaned) with head and tail intact
1 tablespoon	salt
	water
1 teaspoon	vegetable oil
1 tablespoon	peanut oil
2	¼-inch slices peeled and minced fresh ginger root*
4 small cloves	garlic, peeled and crushed
3	green onions, including tops, cut in 1-inch pieces
2 tablespoons	dry sherry
¼ cup	soy sauce
1 tablespoon	toasted sesame seeds

Rinse and dry fish with absorbent paper; salt it. Place fish on heat proof plate. Place on rack in roaster. Add enough water to roaster pan to come to one inch below fish. Set roaster on heat on top of stove. Bring water to boil. Meanwhile, heat oil in a small skillet. Add peanut oil, ginger root, garlic and chopped green onions; cook 30 seconds. Add sherry and soy sauce, stir. Cover roaster and let water boil 15 minutes or until fish is done. Add skillet ingredients. Serve hot. The roaster may be placed in oven instead of stovetop.
Serves 4.

Heck Of A Hekka
(Beef, Pork, Shrimp or Chicken)

I was first introduced to this exotic dish in Hilo, Hawaii at the home of a lovely Japanese couple. It was love at first taste. And it has been a favorite since.

Mae

2 tablespoons	peanut oil
4	boneless chicken breasts, cut into 1½ inch pieces
1 cup	water
1½ ounces	Japanese Sake* or sherry (optional)
2	medium onions, halved and sliced into thin rings
2 cups	bamboo shoots*, sliced thin
2 cups	fresh mushrooms, sliced
1 block	tofu*, cut in small cubes
¾ cup	soy sauce
6 tablespoons	brown sugar
½ teaspoon	monosodium glutamate
2 cups	green onions, cut into 2 inch lengths
1 (20 ounce) box	frozen broccoli flowerets

Heat oil in wok or large skillet. Add chicken and fry. Add water and wine and cook chicken for 15 minutes. Add onions, bamboo shoots, mushrooms and tofu. Then add soy sauce, sugar, monosodium glutamate and cook without stirring for 10 minutes, until sauce begins to boil. Then add green onions and broccoli and cook for 2 to 3 minutes. (Green vegetables should be added last so as not to overcook.)

Other greens such as fresh spinach, watercress, celery, cabbage, field cress, or bean sprouts may be substituted. Canned mushrooms may be used; and if this is done, use the juice in the mushroom can instead of water.

This popular dish is ideal for serving to guests savoring Japanese food for the first time. Arrange the chicken and vegetable ingredients attractively on a platter, remembering to place those ingredients to be cooked first toward the outside of the platter. Electric skillets can be used and this dish can be cooked directly at the table. You may also use a heavy skillet and cook this dish over a hibachi. It adds a novel and unique touch to your dinners. The tantalizing aroma of the food being cooked will whet your appetite. Have a pot of hot rice and tea ready and what a meal! What a party!
Serves 6.

Fish Teriyaki

3 pounds	fish fillets
¾ cup	teriyaki marinating sauce
½ teaspoon	peeled crushed fresh ginger root*
2 stalks	fresh green onions, chopped diagonally
½ teaspoon	brown sugar

Place fillets on lightly greased broiler pan a few inches from heat. Combine teriyaki sauce with ginger root, green onions, and brown sugar. Brush with sauce and broil 3 to 4 minutes per side or until fish flakes easily. Baste often. Just before serving, heat a little sauce and pour over each fillet.
Serves 4.

Maiau Seafood Symphony

½ pound	scallops
1 teaspoon	salt
1 cup	water
½ pint	oysters
1 cup	shrimp
3 tablespoons	butter
1 cup	mushrooms
1½ tablespoons	finely chopped green onion
3 tablespoons	flour
½ cup	thin cream
2 teaspoons	sherry
2 teaspoons	lemon juice
1 cup	bread crumbs
1 tablespoon	melted butter
½ cup	grated cheese
	dash of paprika
1 tablespoon	parsley flakes

Cut the scallops into small cubes, add one-half teaspoon salt and the water and simmer for 15 minutes. Drain scallops, reserving stock. Drain oysters, reserving liquid. Cook and drain shrimp, reserving liquid. Combine scallop stock, oyster liquid and shrimp stock to make 1 cup liquid. If more liquid is needed for the cup, add milk. Heat butter, add mushrooms and onion. Cook over low heat for about 5 minutes. Blend in flour and slowly add seafood liquid. Cook until thickened, stirring constantly. Add cream, sherry, lemon juice, remaining salt and seafood. Place the mixture into a baking dish. Sprinkle with a crumbled mixture of bread crumbs, melted butter and cheese. Sprinkle with paprika and parsley flakes. Broil for a few minutes until mixture is browned and bubbly.
Serves 6-8.

Secret Shrimp Fried Rice

If you can keep a secret, you can make a big hit with this recipe. Place a carry out order for about 2 pints of Shrimp Fried Rice at a good Oriental resturant. This rice already contains the spices and exotic flavoring you need. The rice is the right kind . . . not sticky. Take the order home, follow the directions below, and everyone will wonder about the secret of this great fried rice.

½ pound	bacon, cut into 1 inch slices
4	eggs, beaten
2 tablespoons	soy sauce
1 pound	fresh shrimp, boiled, shelled, and cut up
4 stalks	green onions, cut into 1 inch slices
2 pints	Shrimp Fried Rice

Cook bacon in a skillet until almost done; set aside. Pour out bacon fat. Pour beaten eggs into skillet and cook omelet style until firm and brown; turn and cook other side. Remove from skillet onto cutting board and slice into 1 inch strips; set aside. Add soy sauce to skillet. Cook shrimp and onions in soy sauce 1 minute. Add all these in-gredients to the order of Shrimp Fried Rice; including the soy sauce used to cook shrimp and onions. Toss well. To warm, place fried rice into an electric wok and set on warm, or keep warm on the stove. Also warms well in microwave. Great covered dish for a party. . . add a salad and you've got a meal. This recipe can be easily halved or doubled.
Serves 12-16.

Chicken Breasts In Oriental Sauce

6	boneless chicken breasts
5 cups	water
½ teaspoon	fresh peeled ginger root*, crushed
½ cup	sugar
2½ teaspoons	salt
2 tablespoons	soy sauce
3 tablespoons	sherry
2 tablespoons	oyster sauce*
1 teaspoon	peeled and grated ginger root*
¼ teaspoon	Five Spices*
½ cup	soup stock
1 teaspoon	monosodium glutamate
2	medium Irish potatoes, cut in half lengthwise

Place chicken with 5 cups of water and ginger root in a medium pot and cook for 25 minutes. Drain and save ½ cup of the stock. Set aside chicken in a bowl, blend together remaining ingredients except potatoes, making a sauce. Place boiled chicken in pot and add potatoes. Pour the sauce over and simmer for 20 minutes, stirring once or twice.
Serves 6.

Shoyu Chicken

1 teaspoon	monosodium glutamate
¼ cup	corn oil
¼ cup	soy sauce

¼ cup   sugar
1 clove   garlic, crushed
½ teaspoon   peeled, grated ginger
root*
8   broiler fryer chicken
thighs

Mix together all ingredients except chicken. Place chicken thighs in pan, pour sauce over chicken and bake at 325 degrees for 1 hour, turning chicken twice during baking. Skim fat from sauce, if desired. Serve sauce with chicken.
Serves 2-4.

Diamondhead Prime Rib Roast

1 (8-10 pound)   rib roast
garlic salt
seasoning salt
black pepper
white pepper
1 (8 ounce) can   spiced apple rings,
drained
fresh parsley sprigs

Sprinkle roast on all sides with garlic salt, seasoning salt, black pepper, white pepper; knead into meat (do not punch holes into your roast). Place roast, fat side up, on a rack in a roasting pan. Insert a meat thermometer, making sure the bulb does not touch fat or bone. Bake, uncovered, at 325 degrees, approximately 3 to 4 hours. Remove from oven. Trim fat from roast if desired, then bake 10 minutes at 400 degrees or until browned. Slice roast and place slices on a hot serving platter. Garnish with spiced apple rings and parsley.

Note: Bake roast to an internal temperature of 150 degrees for medium rare and 160 degrees for medium.
Serves 12-16.

Mu Shu Pork

Although this dish is traditionally served with Mandarin Pancakes, it is also very delicious just served with plain rice.

½ pound	boneless pork fillet
2 full	cloud ear mushrooms*
⅓ cup	dried lily buds*
2	green onions, including tops
2	eggs
3 tablespoons	oil
½ teaspoon	salt
1 teaspoon	sugar
1 cup	sliced bamboo shoots*
2 tablespoons	soy sauce
¼ cup	chicken broth

Cut pork on the diagonal into slices ¼-inch thick, 1½ to 2 inches long. Wash cloud ear mushrooms very thoroughly. Soak in warm water for 30 minutes. Wash again, drain, remove stems, and cut into ¼-inch strips. Wash lily buds and soak for 1 hour in warm water. Wash again, drain, and cut off any hard ends. Mince green onions. Beat eggs lightly.

Heat 1½ tablespoons of the oil and ½ teaspoon salt in skillet. Add pork slices and stir-fry for 1 minute. Add sugar, mushrooms, lily buds, bamboo shoots, and soy sauce. Mix well and stir-fry for 1 minute. Remove. Clean pan. Add the other 1½ tablespoons of oil, and scramble the eggs till very firm, breaking the eggs up into small pieces. Add the pork mixture and mix well. Add the broth; and stir and cook for 1 minute. Add the minced green onions and mix well. *Serves 4-6.*

Mandarin Pancakes

Leftover pancakes can be frozen in foil. French crêpes are an acceptable substitute

> 1 cup   water
> 2 cups   unsifted all-purpose
>   flour
>   sesame oil*
>   vegetable oil

Boil the water. Place flour in a bowl and make a well in the center. Add ¾ cup of the water, beating hard with a wooden spoon. You may need to add more water if the consistency is not correct, but the dough should not be too sticky. Turn out on lightly floured board and knead until smooth and firm, adding flour as needed. This will take about 5 minutes. Put the kneaded dough into a clean bowl, cover with a towel, and let stand for 1 hour. Turn out on lightly floured board and knead again very briefly. Make a sausage-shaped roll about 1½ inches in diameter. Using your fingers, divide into 18 equal-sized pieces. Make each into a round ball. Now with your fingers, flatten each ball to about ¼-inch thickness. Brush the tops lightly with the sesame oil. Put two flattened balls together, with oiled sides together. Place these on a lightly floured board and with a rolling pin, roll out as thin as you can, keeping each pair together and as uniform and circular as possible. The reason the pancakes are rolled out in pairs is to have them paper-thin and pliable when finished.

Using a little vegetable oil, lightly oil and heat a flat skillet until medium hot. Fry pancakes one pair at a time about 1 minute on each side. They should be light golden without brown spots.

Nancy Maynard

Puka Burgers

Puka means hole in Hawaiian.

4 pounds	lean ground beef
	selected condiments in
	small containers:
	chopped onions
	chopped pickles
	relish
	cheese sauce
	ketchup
	mustard
	crushed pineapple
	lettuce, to garnish
	tomatoes, to garnish
	salt and pepper to taste

Preheat broiler. Take 4 to 5 ounces of meat at a time and shape into 12 patties, leaving a hole in the center of each. Place on broiler. When cooked to desired doneness, place on hot buns and let each person select their own condiments and put into the puka (hole). If desired, garnish with slices of tomato and lettuce. Kids especially enjoy filling the puka and gives your hamburger a new zest.
Serves 12-16.

Spareribs Pacifica

3 pounds	spareribs
	flour
	oil
1 (6 ounce) can	orange juice
	concentrate,
	thawed and undiluted
¾ cup	water

            1 teaspoon   salt
            2 cloves   garlic, peeled and
                           chopped
            1 teaspoon   monosodium glutamate

Coat spareribs with flour. Heat oil in a large skillet and brown spareribs. To the skillet, add orange juice concentrate, water, salt, garlic and monsodium glutamate; simmer for 1 hour or until meat is tender.
Serves 3-4.

Chi Chi Beef

        2 tablespoons   peanut oil
                   4   green onions, cut in
                          1-inch pieces
        1 tablespoon   peeled and minced
                          fresh ginger root*
            1 pound   boneless beef chuck, cut
                          in 1-inch cubes
            ¼ cup   sugar
        2 tablespoons   soy sauce
            ⅓ cup   dry sherry
            1 cup   water
            ½ teaspoon dried red pepper flakes

Heat oil in skillet or wok. Add onions and ginger root, stir-fry 1 minute. Add beef; stir-fry 2 minutes or until brown. Mix together sugar, soy sauce, sherry, water and red pepper flakes until sugar dissolves. Add to wok. Lower heat and simmer for 30 minutes. Uncover, increase heat to high, cook until sauce thickens, another 30 minutes. Remove from skillet or wok. Serve hot with picks to spear meat.
Makes approximately 40 pieces.

Polynesian Oysters

Abalone is used in Hawaii instead of oysters. Abalone is quite a delicacy in the Islands.

10	large fresh mushrooms
½ pint	fresh oysters
½ cup	chicken stock
½ pound	pork, sliced in strips
1 piece	peeled ginger root*, sliced
1 (8 ounce) can	water chestnuts*, sliced
1 teaspoon	sugar
1 tablespoon	sherry or whiskey
1 tablespoon	oyster sauce*
2 teaspoons	cornstarch
2 tablespoons	water

Wash mushrooms and slice. Drain oysters, reserving liquid. Combine chicken stock and oyster liquid to make 1 cup liquid; simmer for 5 minutes. Add pork and ginger, cook 10 minutes. Add mushrooms and water chestnuts and cook an additional 10 minutes. Add sugar, liquor, and oyster sauce. Add cornstarch which has been dissolved in 2 tablespoons water. Add oysters just before serving. Garnish with Chinese parsley.
Serves 4-6.

Stuffed Flounder Nani Kai (Beautiful Ocean)

6 pounds	fresh flounder
½ teaspoon	garlic salt
¼ teaspoon	black pepper
1-2 cloves	garlic, minced
	vegetable oil

1 (8-ounce) can   scallops, drained and
                 sliced
1 (8-ounce) can   crabmeat, drained
          1   onion, diced
   8-12 ounces   fresh mushrooms, sliced
        ¼ cup   white wine
     1⅓ cups   mayonnaise
              paprika

Preheat oven to 375 degrees. Clean fish for baking. Season with garlic salt and pepper. Set aside. In a frying pan or large saucepan, brown garlic in a small amount of vegetable oil. Add scallops, crabmeat, onion and mushrooms. Just before mushrooms are fully cooked, add wine. Continue cooking for 1 to 2 minutes. Remove from heat. Place mixture in a large mixing bowl, retaining a minimum of liquid. Mix thoroughly with mayonnaise. Place fish in a lightly greased baking pan. Pour mixture over fish. Sprinkle with paprika and bake uncovered for 30 to 35 minutes.
Serves 6-8.

Laulau

   ½ pound   butterfish or salmon
   1 pound   pork butt
      16   luau leaves* or 2
            pounds fresh spinach
       8   ti leaves*

Cut fish into 4 pieces and soak in water for 1 hour. Cut pork butt into 4 pieces. Prepare luau leaves by stripping off outer skin of stem and leaf veins. Wash and remove tough ribs from ti leaves. Lay 2 ti leaves on cutting board. place 4 luau leaves in center. Place a piece of pork and a piece of fish on luau leaves. Fold luau leaves over meat and fish to form a bundle. Tie ends of ti leaves and steam for 3 to 4 hours.
Serves 4.

Wiki Wiki (Quick) Wokery

The Chinese brought the wok to Hawaii many generations ago. Now it is used widely among all the nationalities in the Islands. The scents of aromatic spices, vegetables and meats fill the late tropical evenings as skillful hands prepare sumptuous wok dishes for dinner. The dishes are as varied as the nationalities. They are original, wonderful, and wiki wiki (quick).

During the week I use my food processor to cut the fresh vegetables. Thawed, frozen cut vegetables are also convenient. On weekends, Lee or I take the time to cut everything diagonally for a more palatable and attractive meal. Despite the hand chopping, the wok still provides a quick, easy cooking method.

You will get the best results if you use a wok in stir-fry dishes, but a large skillet can be used as well.

Jade Chicken

1	whole chicken breast, boned and cut into 1 inch strips
¼ teaspoon	salt
¼ teaspoon	pepper
1 tablespoon	vegetable oil
2 stalks	celery, cut diagonally
1	onion, sliced
1 cup	snow peas*
½ cup	chicken broth
1 teaspoon	cornstarch
¼ teaspoon	sugar
1 tablespoon	soy sauce

Season chicken with salt and pepper. Sauté in oil for 1 minute, or until tender. Add vegetables and 2 tablespoons chicken broth. Cover and steam for 1½ minutes. Remove cover and stir once. In a small bowl, mix cornstarch, sugar, soy sauce, and remaining broth. Mix well. Add to chicken and vegetable mixture. Cook and stir for 1 minute, or until mixture thickens. Serve with hot cooked rice.
Serves 6.

Aloha Pepper Steak

This one is for you, Mark.

1 tablespoon	cornstarch
2 tablespoons	peanut oil
1 pound	round steak, thinly sliced and cut in 1½ inch long strips
2	small onions, peeled and each cut into 6 wedges
2	green peppers, cored, seeded and cut into thin 1½ inch long strips
½ cup	fresh mushrooms, thinly sliced
3 tablespoons	soy sauce
1 tablespoon	monosodium glutamate

Mix cornstarch with 2 tablespoons cold water and set aside. Heat oil in skillet or wok until hot. Add meat and stir-fry 3 minutes. Add onions and peppers; stir-fry 2 minutes. Add mushrooms and stir-fry 1 minute. Add next 2 ingredients and stir-fry 1 minute. Remove from heat and drain gravy into another container. Keep warm over low heat. Stir cornstarch mixture; add to gravy; stir until gravy thickens slightly. Remove from heat and pour over steak.
Serves 4.

Stir-Fried Shrimp With Macadamia Nuts

	½ pound	shrimp
(A):	2 teaspoons	cornstarch
	¼ teaspoon	salt
	½	egg white
	½ teaspoon	sherry
		oil for deep fat frying (3 inches deep)
	6 (1 inch) sections	green onions
	6 slices	peeled ginger root*, ¼-inch each slice
	¼ cup	diced bamboo shoots*
(B):	½ teaspoon	cornstarch
	¼ teaspoon	salt
	¼ teaspoon	black pepper
	1 tablespoon	water
	½ teaspoon	sherry
	¼ teaspoon	sesame oil*
	¼ teaspoon	monosodium glutamate, optional
	1 (3½ ounce) jar	Mauna Loa® Bits O' Macadamia Nuts*

Remove shells from shrimp; rinse and devein. Combine shrimp with mixture (A) of cornstarch, salt, egg white and sherry. Marinate shrimp for 20 minutes. Heat oil in a wok to medium-hot. Deep fry shrimp for 30 seconds. Remove shrimp and pour off all but 1 tablespoon of oil from wok; reheat. Stir-fry green onions and ginger for 2 to 3 minutes. Add shrimp, bamboo shoots and mixture (B) of cornstarch, salt, black pepper, water, sherry, sesame oil and monosodium glutamate. Toss ingredients lightly to mix. Add macadamia nuts. Stir-fry until the macadamia nuts are heated through. Serve immediately.
Serves 2-4.

Beef Sukiyaki

4 pounds	top round or sirloin steak
1 pound	Japanese long rice*
8	fresh mushrooms
1½ cups	water
1 (8 ounce) can	bamboo shoots,* sliced
2	large onions, sliced into thin rings
1 bunch	green onions
3 blocks	tofu,* cut in small cubes
3 bunches	watercress or spinach
½ cup	soy sauce
⅓ cup	Sake* or dry sherry
¼ cup	brown sugar
1½ teaspoons	monosodium glutamate
⅔ cups	beef broth
	vegetable oil

Cut steak against the grain into thin strips, 2 inches long. Soak Japanese long rice in water until soft. Drain water and cut long rice in half, discarding the string. Cut watercress into 2 inch strips. Arrange all the vegetables and meat on 2 large platters. Mix together the rest of the spices and liquids. In a wok or frying pan at the table, heat a little oil. Fry half of the steak, onions and mushrooms. Cook over a brisk fire for a few minutes. Sprinkle with sugar mixture. Use only half as this will make 2 batches. Now add bamboo shoots and cook for 2 minutes, stirring frequently. Add tofu, watercress and green onions. Add Japanese long rice. Baste some sauce over greens. Cover and serve as soon as the watercress wilts. Repeat for a second batch. To be a relaxed hostess, cut all vegetables, slice meat, arrange on platter, cover and refrigerate ahead of time. Mix broth. Let your guests cook the sukiyaki at the table.
Serves 6.

Bird Of Paradise

1 (20 ounce) can	Dole® Sliced Pineapple in Syrup
2	whole chicken breasts, split (or fryer, cut up, about 3 pounds)
2 tablespoons	butter
¼ cup	dry sherry
3 tablespoons	soy sauce
2 large cloves	garlic, pressed
2 tablespoons	chopped crystallized ginger
½ teaspoon	salt
1	red bell pepper, seeded, chunked
1½ cups	sliced celery
½ cup	sliced green onion
1	papaya,* peeled, sliced (optional)
1 tablespoon	cornstarch
½ cup	water

Drain pineapple, reserving syrup. Brown chicken in butter. Drain excess fat. Combine reserved syrup with next 5 ingredients; pour over chicken. Cover, simmer 30 minutes, turning chicken once. Remove chicken to platter. Add pineapple, bell pepper, celery, green onion and papaya to pan. Dissolve cornstarch in ½ cup water. Stir into pan juices. Cook until mixture boils and thickens. Spoon over chicken. *Serves 4.*

Oriental Pork And Bok Choy

3 tablespoons	soy sauce
1 tablespoon	packed light brown sugar
1 teaspoon	salt
½ teaspoon	monosodium glutamate
½ teaspoon	peeled and minced ginger root*
3 tablespoons	oil
1 pound	lean pork 1-inch cubes
1	small green pepper, cored, seeded and cut in thin 1 inch long strips
1	small onion, peeled and cut into very thin wedges
4 cups	loosely packed shredded bok choy*
½ cup	cold water
1 tablespoon	cornstarch mixed with
2 teaspoons	cold water

Mix first 5 ingredients; set aside. Heat oil in wok until hot. Add pork; stir-fry 3 minutes. Add pepper and onion; stir-fry 1 minute. Add soy sauce mixture, bok choy and water; toss to combine; cover; cook 1 minute. Uncover; stir cornstarch mixture; add to wok; stir-fry until slightly thickened. Serve immediately.
Serves 4.

Honolulu Hot And Spicy Beef

1 pound	sirloin steak, thinly sliced across grain and cut in 1½ inch long strips
1	egg, lightly beaten
1 teaspoon	baking soda
3 tablespoons	peanut oil
1 tablespoon	cornstarch mixed with
1 tablespoon	cold water
2 tablespoons	peanut oil
1	small red pepper, cored, seeded and cut into thin 1½ inch long strips
1	small green pepper, cored, seeded and cut into thin 1½ inch long strips
1 (8 ounce) can	bamboo shoots*, drained
1 tablespoon	dry sherry
2	small dried chilis, crushed
1 tablespoon	soy sauce
½ teaspoon	sugar
½ teaspoon	salt
¼ teaspoon	sesame oil*
1 tablespoon	cornstarch mixed with
1 tablespoon	cold water

Mix meat with next 4 ingredients in small bowl; set aside to marinate at least 20 minutes. Heat oil in wok until hot. Add meat mixture; stir-fry 1 minute. Add next 3 ingredients; stir-fry 1 minute. Add next 6 ingredients; stir-fry 1 minute. Stir cornstarch mixture; add to wok. Stir-fry until sauce thickens. Serve immediately.
Serves 4-6.

Wiki Wiki Walnut Chicken

½ cup	water
2 tablespoons	cornstarch
1 tablespoon	soy sauce
½ teaspoon	sugar
½ teaspoon	salt
3 tablespoons	oil
1 cup	walnut halves
1	whole chicken breast, split, skinned, boned and slivered
1 (10 ounce) box	frozen broccoli, thawed
12	fresh mushrooms, wiped clean and sliced
½ cup	sliced water chestnuts*, drained
½ cup	sliced bamboo shoots*, drained

Mix first 5 ingredients; set aside. Heat 1 tablespoon oil in wok; add walnuts; stir-fry 1 minute. Do not let burn. Remove walnuts with strainer; drain on paper towel. Discard oil in wok. Heat remaining 2 tablespoons oil in wok until hot. Add chicken; stir-fry 3 minutes. Add next 4 ingredients; stir-fry 3 minutes. Add cornstarch mixture; cook until thickened. Serve immediately, topped with walnuts.
Serves 4.

Smart And Sassy Shrimp

2 (¼-inch) slices	peeled fresh ginger root*
1 large clove	garlic, peeled
2 tablespoons	soy sauce
1 tablespoon	dry sherry
2 tablespoons	ketchup
1 teaspoon	sugar
¼ teaspoon	red pepper (optional)
2 tablespoons	peanut oil
1 pound	raw shrimp, shelled, deveined and patted dry
2	green onions, including tops, cut diagonally in 1-inch pieces

Mince ginger root and garlic; set aside. Mix soy sauce, sherry, ketchup red pepper and sugar; set aside. Heat oil in wok or skillet until hot. Add ginger root and garlic, stir and cook a few seconds. Add shrimp, cook while stirring for 3 minutes or until pink. Add green onion, cook 30 seconds, add soy sauce mixture, cook 30 seconds. Stir only enough to blend ingredients and serve immediately.
Serves 4.

Aloha Barbecued Fish

1 (4-5 pound)	fish
2 tablespoons	salad oil
2 tablespoons	vinegar
½ cup	ketchup
¼ cup	water
½ cup	chopped onion

1 clove	garlic, minced
2 drops	hot pepper sauce
2 tablespoons	Worcestershire sauce
1 teaspoon	salt
¼ teaspoon	pepper
¼ teaspoon	dry mustard
½ teaspoon	chili powder
1 (6-ounce) can	mushrooms

Place cleaned fish in foil. Combine the rest of the ingredients in a saucepan and heat. Pour sauce over fish and bake in a 375 degree oven for 25 to 30 minutes.
Serves 2-4.

Hawaiian Short Ribs

6 pounds	short ribs
1½ cups	soy sauce
¼ cup	water
½ cup	sugar
½ teaspoon	monosodium glutamate
1 (1 inch) piece	peeled ginger root, mashed
3 tablespoons	brandy or bourbon
1 clove	garlic, mashed

In a large pot, cover short ribs with water and boil for 25 minutes. Remove from heat and let cool. Drain meat and dry. Mix other ingredients in a deep narrow bowl, add short ribs and marinate for 10 to 15 minutes. Grill ribs about 5 inches above hot coals for 15 to 20 minutes or until golden brown and crispy.
Serves 6.

Teriyaki Chicken

¾ cup	soy sauce
¾ cup	brown sugar
2 tablespoons	sherry
1 tablespoon	sesame oil*
1 tablespoon	sesame seeds
½ teaspoon	monosodium glutamate
1 clove	garlic, minced
1½ teaspoons	peeled and crushed fresh ginger root*
3-4 pounds	chicken thighs or drumsticks

Mix all ingredients except chicken. Soak chicken 4 hours or overnight in sauce. Drain chicken. Bake in shallow pan for 1 hour at 325 degrees. Turn pieces over and baste with sauce often. Ten minutes before turning heat off, pour the rest of the soy sauce mixture on top. Serve with chopped green onion and Chinese parsley.
Serves 10-12.

Deluxe Crabmeat Chowder

1 pound	deluxe white crabmeat
2 cups	water
2 cups	diced potatoes
3 slices	bacon, chopped
1	onion, chopped
2 cups	milk
	salt, pepper and butter
	to taste

Place crabmeat in a saucepan; add water. Bring to a simmer and cook 1 minute. Remove crabmeat, reserving stock. Add potatoes to the stock; cook until tender, but still firm. Meanwhile, fry bacon in a skillet; stir in onion and cook until translucent. Add bacon, onion, crabmeat and milk to the potatoes. Season with salt, pepper and butter.
Serves 4.

Oven Kalua Pork

1 (5-7 pound)	pork butt
2 tablespoons	Hawaiian salt* or rock salt
4 tablespoons	liquid smoke
10-12	ti leaves*

Cut 1½ inch slits around pork and rub surface with Hawaiian salt. Brown pork on all sides. Brush with liquid smoke. Wrap pork in ti leaves and tie with string. Wrap again in aluminum foil and seal tightly. Bake at 350 degrees for 1 hour then lower heat to 325 degrees and bake for 3 hours.
Serves 8-10.

Spicy Orange Chicken

2	whole chicken breasts, split, skinned, boned and cut in 1 inch cubes
1 teaspoon	salt
1	egg, lightly beaten
2 tablespoons	cornstarch
5 tablespoons	peanut oil, divided
2 tablespoons	soy sauce
1 tablespoon	sugar
1 teaspoon	sesame oil*
1 tablespoon	dry sherry
1 teaspoon	white vinegar
	grated peel from 2 small oranges
¼ teaspoon	dried red pepper flakes
4	¼-inch slices fresh ginger root,* peeled and coarsely chopped
3 stalks	green onions, cut diagonally in ¼ inch slices
1 teaspoon	monosodium glutamate

Mix chicken, salt, egg, 1 tablespoon cornstarch and 1 tablespoon oil in bowl until chicken is coated; set aside. Mix next 5 ingredients and remaining 1 tablespoon cornstarch; set aside. Heat 3 tablespoons oil in wok until hot. Stir-fry chicken until opaque, about 3 minutes. Remove with strainer; set aside. Heat 1 tablespoon oil in wok until hot; add orange peel and red pepper flakes. Cook until blackened, about 10 seconds, stirring constantly. Add ginger root, green onions, monosodium glutamate and chicken; stir-fry 10 seconds. Stir soy mixture; add to wok; stir-fry 1 minute. Serve immediately.
Serves 4.

Ono Lemon Chicken

Ladies, this is a great luncheon entrée.

1 pound	boned chicken
½ teaspoon	salt
1 tablespoon	sherry or Sake*
1 tablespoon	soy sauce
½ teaspoon	sugar
2	eggs
¼ cup	cornstarch
½ teaspoon	baking powder
2 cups	vegetable oil for frying
1 tablespoon	vegetable oil
1 teaspoon	salt
3 tablespoons	sugar
1 tablespoon	cornstarch
1-2 tablespoons	lemon juice
1 cup	canned chicken broth
1-2	lemons, thinly sliced for garnish

Cut chicken in bite-sized pieces. Combine salt, sherry or Sake, soy sauce and sugar. Marinate chicken for 20 minutes. Beat eggs; add cornstarch and baking powder. Beat to form a smooth batter. Heat oil to 375 degrees. Coat chicken pieces with batter and deep-fry for 4 to 5 minutes or until well browned. Drain on absorbent paper. Make lemon sauce by heating oil and slowly adding salt, sugar, cornstarch, lemon juice and chicken broth. Stir constantly until sauce is clear. Pour sauce over chicken. Garnish with lemon slices. Serve over hot Chinese cabbage or broccoli.
Serves 3-4.

Honolulu City Chicken On A Stick

5-6	boneless chicken breasts
¼ cup	soy sauce
1 clove	garlic, crushed
3 tablespoons	sugar
1 tablespoon	sherry
2 tablespoons	cornstarch
¼ teaspoon	monosodium glutamate
2	medium onions
2	bell peppers
1 (8-ounce) can	button mushrooms
1	large eggplant
1 (16-ounce) can	chunk pineapple
	corn oil
2 dozen	bamboo barbecue sticks
1¼ cups	flour
1¼ cups	cornstarch
¼ teaspoon	salt
¼ teaspoon	monosodium glutamate
1	egg
¾ cup	flat beer

Cut chicken breasts into bite-sized chunks. Combine soy sauce, garlic, sugar, sherry, cornstarch and monosodium glutamate and marinate chicken in sauce for 1 hour. Cut onion in eighths, being careful to keep layers together. Cut peppers into eighths. Drain mushrooms. Cut eggplant into 1-inch cubes and soak in water for about 15 minutes. Drain pineapple. After chicken has been marinated, skewer chicken, vegetables, and pineapple onto bamboo sticks. Heat oil to about 375 degrees. Combine flour, cornstarch, salt, monosodium glutamate, egg and beer. Dip chicken sticks in batter and deep fry in hot oil until batter is browned nicely. Turn over and continue browning. Drain on paper towels. Serve warm or cold. Center cut pork alternated with veal may be used in the place of chicken.
Makes 16-24 skewers.

Lee's Teriyaki Style Steak

This one is for Lessie, George, David, Michelle and Tina.

2½ pounds   sirloin tip roast
2 (10 ounce) bottles   teriyaki marinating
sauce
1 tablespoon   peeled and crushed
fresh gingeroot
5 stalks   finely chopped green
onions, including
leafy tops
1 tablespoon   brown sugar

Place roast on a chopping board and cut into thin strips, approximately ⅛ inch thick by 1½ inch wide by 3 inches, or half the size of a strip of bacon. In a large bowl combine the teriyaki sauce, crushed ginger root, chopped green onions, and brown sugar. Stir until well blended. Place the sirloin strips into the marinating sauce, making sure all of the strips are well saturated. Marinate no less than 3 hours or marinate overnight, in refrigerator. When ready to serve, lift meat strips out of sauce with fork and set sauce aside. Cook strips over hot charcoals until brown and done. Pour sauce into saucepan and heat, or keep warm until ready to serve. Pour sauce over meat servings and serve with hot rice.

Do not overcook meat.

If cutting roast at home, it is easier to slice if roast is partially frozen. Or simply ask your butcher to cut it for you at time of purchase. *Serves 6-8.*

The Dole Super Burger

1 (20 ounce) can	Dole® Crushed Pineapple in Juice
3 pounds	ground beef
3	eggs
2 cloves	garlic, pressed
1 cup	cubed Cheddar cheese
¾ cup	chopped onion
½ cup	bread crumbs
½ teaspoon	crushed red pepper flakes
1 (6 ounce) can	Dole® Pineapple Juice
½ cup	orange marmalade
¼ cup	honey
2 tablespoons	cornstarch
1 tablespoon	Worcestershire sauce
1	large round loaf French bread

Drain pineapple well, reserving juice. Combine pineapple, beef, eggs, garlic, cheese, onion, bread crumbs and pepper flakes. Mix well. On a broiler rack, shape meat into a large patty to fit bread. In a saucepan, combine reserved pineapple juice with remaining ingredients, except bread. Cook, stirring, until sauce boils and thickens. Brush sauce over burger. Broil 4 inches from heat 20 minutes, basting after first 10 minutes. Using large spatula, place burger on a plate. Invert onto another plate, uncooked side up. Slide onto broiler rack. Baste; broil 10 minutes longer. Serve burger on bread. Garnish as desired. Cut into 6 to 8 servings.
Serves 6-8.

Succulent Steamed Fish With Vegetables

Fish is almost always steamed in Hawaii and topped off with a piping hot spicy mixture.

1 pound	fish fillets
1½ teaspoons	salt
2 cups	shredded bok choy*
1 small piece	peeled, minced fresh ginger root*
1 clove	garlic, minced
2	green onions, minced
1	fresh tomato, sliced
½ bunch	watercress, cut in small pieces
3 tablespoons	soy sauce
	pepper
	monosodium glutamate
¼ cup	sesame oil*

Clean and prepare fish fillets. Knead salt into fish. Steam fish until done, about 15 to 20 minutes. Arrange 1 cup bok choy on a platter. Place fish on top. Season fish with ginger and garlic. Place other cup of bok choy, green onions, tomato and watercress over fish. Sprinkle with salt and pepper and monosodium glutamate. In a saucepan, heat oil until very hot, pour over fish.
Serves 6.

Chicken With Long Rice

2 or 3 pounds	fryer chicken or thighs, chopped in serving pieces
6	large fresh mushrooms, sliced
1 bundle	long rice*, soaked until soft (cut 3 inches long)
3 stalks	green onion, cut in 2 inch lengths
2 tablespoons	oil
1 clove	garlic, crushed
½ teaspoon	ginger root*, peeled and crushed
½ teaspoon	monosodium glutamate
½ teaspoon	curry powder
1 quart	water
½ teaspoon	black pepper (optional)

Heat oil in a heavy pot. Add ginger root, garlic and chicken and stir-fry until light brown. Add water and mushrooms. Cook until tender, about 45 minutes. Add salt, curry, and monosodium glutamate and cook for 15 minutes. Add long rice, green onion and simmer for 10 minutes.

Serves 6-8.

Chanko Nabe Takasago Beya (Sumo Wrestler's Dinner)

3-4 slices	fresh salmon
1	daikon*
1	carrot
2-3	cabbage leaves
1-2	onions
1 bunch	spinach
6 cups	milk
1 tablespoon	butter
¾ cup	Sake*
2 tablespoons	sugar
2 tablespoons	soy sauce
½ teaspoon	monosodium glutamate
1 (8 ounce) can	bamboo shoots*, drained

Cut salmon into bite sized pieces. Cut daikon and carrot into diagonal chunks and parboil. Cut cabbage into 2-inch squares and onion into ½ inch slices. Tear spinach into 2-inch lengths. Pour milk into large pot. Add butter, Sake, sugar, soy sauce and monosodium glutamate. When milk comes to a boil, add remaining ingredients except salmon and spinach. When first vegetables are cooked, add salmon and spinach. *Serves 1 Sumo Wrestler or 4-6 average people.*

Ribs In Pineapple-Mustard Sauce

3 pounds	pork spareribs
½ teaspoon	salt
½ teaspoon	garlic powder
¼ teaspoon	pepper
2 tablespoons	butter
1	small onion, chopped
¼ cup	packed brown sugar
¼ cup	Dijon mustard
¼ cup	dry white wine
2 cups	chopped Dole® fresh pineapple
2 tablespoons	chopped parsley

Place ribs on rack in baking pan. Sprinkle with salt, garlic powder and pepper. Roast in 375 degree oven about 45 minutes. Remove to baking dish. Melt butter in skillet and sauté onion until tender. Stir in sugar, mustard and wine. Boil rapidly about 2 minutes to reduce slightly. Stir in pineapple and spoon sauce over ribs. Bake in 375 degree oven 15 minutes. Sprinkle with parsley.
Serves 4-6.

Char Siu Spareribs

4 pounds	spareribs
⅛ teaspoon	Five Spices*
2 teaspoons	Hoisin Sauce*
1 teaspoon	meat coloring or ½ teaspoon red food coloring
1¼ cups	brown sugar
1 cup	soy sauce

Boil spareribs for about 1 hour. Mix remaining ingredients for sauce and soak boiled spareribs in sauce for 1 to 2 hours. Bake in oven at 325 degrees for one hour or grill until browned.
Serves 4.

Sunset Snapper

Opakapaka, kumu, mullet or papio are some of the Island fish prepared this way.

3 to 5 pounds	red snapper
1½ teaspoons	salt
	dash of pepper
1 tablespoon	minced onion
1 tablespoon	minced parsley
1 tablespoon	bacon drippings
1 cup	small bread cubes
¼ cup	milk or stock
3 slices	bacon
	cabbage leaves or green corn husks

Select a shallow baking pan large enough for your fish. After fish is clean and prepared for cooking, rub the inside with salt. Combine the next six ingredients. Stuff fish lightly with stuffing; secure with skewers. Place bacon slices over top of fish. Wrap in green corn husks or cabbage leaves. Place fish in prepared pan and bake at 325 degrees for 15 to 20 minutes per pound or until done.
Serves 6-8.

High Surf Seafood Pot

6 tablespoons	oil
4 cloves	garlic, minced
1	large onion, chopped
2 cups	leeks, ½-inch slices
2	large tomatoes, chopped
8 ounces	fresh mushrooms
1 cup	wine
1 tablespoon	monosodium glutamate
2 cups	hot water
¼ teaspoon	saffron
	salt and pepper
12	shrimp, cleaned
12	scallops, washed
1 (8 ounce) can	white crabmeat
12 slices	light meat fish (red snapper, sea bass)

In a large pot, heat oil. Add garlic, onion, leeks, tomatoes, and fresh mushrooms and stir until heated through. Add wine, monosodium glutamate, hot water and saffron; stir until heated through. Add salt and pepper to taste. Add shrimp, scallops, crabmeat and fish. If necessary, add more hot water. Check taste and add salt and pepper as needed.
Serves 8-10.

Lobster Tail Lahaina

2 (1 pound)	fresh lobster tails
1 teaspoon	salt
4 cups	shredded cabbage
4 stalks	celery, cut in paper thin strips
2	onions, cut in paper thin strips
½ teaspoon	salt
¼ teaspoon	pepper
1 cup	mayonnaise
1 tablespoon	lemon juice
½ teaspoon	monosodium glutamate
4 teaspoons	mayonnaise, divided
½ teaspoon	white pepper
	dash of paprika

Wash lobster tails and place into boiling water with 1 teaspoon salt. Cover and cook for 20 minutes. Remove and cool. Remove meat, shred, place into bowl and set aside. In a large bowl, add cabbage, celery, onions, salt, pepper, lemon juice, mayonnaise, and monosodium glutamate. Add lobster meat. Mix well. Place in 4 to 6 lobster shells or individual baking dishes. Top with 1 teaspoon of mayonnaise, white pepper and paprika. Bake in preheated 325 degree oven for 15 minutes.
Serves 4-6.

Fresh Ginger Root

Fresh ginger root is an integral part of Island cookery. It is used in appetizers, vegetables, meats, desserts and preserves.

It has a clean hot taste and aromatic fragrance.

Ginger root is found in the produce section of most large grocery markets. It is easily recognized as a gnarled light brown root—usually located near the fresh garlic or horseradish.

Always peel the portion of root you are planning to use and freeze the rest in a tight container.

Some recipes call for it to be crushed, chopped or minced. In some dishes, such as stir-fry, you may leave the ginger whole and remove it when the dish is cooked.

The taste isn't as distinctive, but you may use the ground ginger found in the spice section or crystallized ginger.

Tempura

Tempura is a Japanese frying technique in which small pieces of vegetables and meats are fried three or four pieces at a time.

Tempura recipes are prepared extensively throughout Hawaii in homes and restaurants.

The secret to this wonderfully versatile dish is in the batter. The really good tempura batter, when cooked, is light, lacy, fluffy, and crunchy. The cooked color is cream, so do not expect the batter to brown.

One person can do this, or you can make a small dinner party of it. If more than one participates, place your wok or electric skillet on the table. Divide batter so that each person has his own.

Tempura Preparations:
1.   Select one, two, three, or more ingredients for tempura frying. Cut into bite-sized pieces or grate. Have at room temperature.
2.   Prepare dipping sauces. You may do this in advance. Serve at room temperature also.
3.   Make the batter of your choice (Beer Batter or Icy Batter).
4.   Heat oil in wok or skillet (electric if preparing at the table). If you do not have a tempura ring, line a plate with absorbent paper for draining excess oil from foods. A large strainer set over a saucepan is good, too.
5.   Using chopsticks or tongs, coat ingredients to be fried in batter, dipping one piece at a time. Then drop into hot oil. Fry only 3 or 4 pieces at a time for about 3 minutes. Increase the temperature of oil as you fry to keep the oil hot enough. Remove food from oil with slotted spoon or tongs and drain.
6.   If more than one person is frying, they should have their own individual batter and dipping sauce.

Suggested Ingredients:
Carrots - **grated or cut into 3-inch strips**
Celery - **cut into 3-inch strips**
Cucumber - **peeled and thinly sliced**
Zucchini - **unpeeled, cut in small strips**
Green Beans - **ends and strings removed, cut into small**

strips
Eggplant - **unpeeled, cut into thin strips**
Parsley Sprigs
Mushrooms - **halved if large**
Onions - **peeled, cut in thin (very thin) slices, keeping rings intact.**
Sweet Potatoes - **peeled, cut in small slices**
Snow Peas*
Fish Fillets - **make sure they are free of bones**
Scallops
Shrimp - **shelled**
Lobster - **bite-sized pieces**
Boneless Chicken - **bite sized pieces**
Chicken Livers
Apple Wedges - **these taste like minature apple tarts**

Dipping Sauces:
Soy Sauce
Lemon Juice
Sweet and Sour Sauce
Hot Mustard Sauce
Light Barbecue Sauce (bottled)

Tempura Beer Batter

2	eggs
1⅓ cups	self-rising flour
1 teaspoon	salt
1 cup	flat beer
3-4 drops	yellow food coloring (optional)

Beat eggs in bowl; add ⅓ cup flour and salt. Add remaining flour alternately with beer, beating after each addition. Let batter stand at room temperature approximately 1 hour.

Tempura batter is white when done. The yellow food coloring adds a light gold cast to batter.

Icy Tempura Batter

⅔ cup	flour
3 tablespoons	cornstarch
½ teaspoon	salt
2	eggs
¾ cup	ice water
2-3 drops	yellow food coloring (optional)

Mix flour, cornstarch and salt together in bowl. Beat eggs and ice water together in a separate bowl until blended. Add to flour mixture; stir until just moistened. The batter will be lumpy. Do not continue to stir. Keep batter cold by placing it in a bowl set in a larger container of crushed ice.

Add yellow food coloring if you want a more yellow batter. Tempura batter is supposed to be white and fluffy.

Papa's Corned Beef Brisket And Lettuce

This recipe came from Lee's father, David Keao Jr. It is so unusual and tasty. When you try it once you'll add it to your favorite recipes.

1 (3-4 pound)	fresh corned beef brisket with seasonings already added
4 large heads	iceberg lettuce, quartered
	prepared mustard

Place brisket in large pan and completely cover with water. Cook on medium heat until it is very tender, approximately 1½ hours per pound. Keep adding hot water to keep the liquid level to the top of the roast. Turn off heat, add lettuce. Let it steep in the brisket liquid for a few minutes to absorb liquid. Do not continue cooking. Slice brisket into servings. Place lightly cooked lettuce on plate and serve with prepared mustard.

Using a pressure cooker cuts the cooking time in half for the brisket. Any leftover liquid and brisket may be refrigerated and heated the next day, adding additional fresh lettuce. Rice tops this off and makes a great meal.

Serves 6.

Sauces And Dips

If you need a zestful departure from the ordinary, like routine salads, condiments, left-overs or salad dressings, then the next few pages could be your answer.

When it comes to "saucing" and "dipping", the Hawaiians are totally uninhibited. They nearly always have a dip on the table or a sauce prepared to bring out the best in foods. So go ahead and "hang loose"!

Surprise your family, friends and yourself with some tropical "punch" from these Aloha sauces and dips.

Koko Dressing

This is great for green salads. You may never buy bottled dressing again.

½ cup	cider vinegar
1 tablespoon	Dijon mustard
1 teaspoon	celery seeds
½ teaspoon	Worcestershire sauce
1	egg
3 teaspoons	sugar
1½ teaspoons	salt
¼ teaspoon	white pepper
1 clove	garlic, crushed
1 teaspoon	sweet pickle relish
½ teaspoon	Kitchen Bouquet
½	lemon
2 cups	vegetable oil

Combine cider vinegar, mustard, celery seeds, Worcestershire sauce, egg, sugar, salt, white pepper, garlic, sweet pickle relish, Kitchen Bouquet, and juice of half a lemon. Slowly blend mixture into oil. Store in your own salad dressing bottles.
Yields 1½ pints.

Honey Dressing For Fruit Salad

⅓ cup	sugar
1 teaspoon	dry mustard
1 teaspoon	paprika
1 teaspoon	celery seeds
¼ teaspoon	salt
⅓ cup	honey
5 tablespoons	vinegar
1 tablespoon	lemon juice
1 teaspoon	onion juice
1 cup	salad oil

Mix well and pour over fruit salad.
Yields 1⅔ cups.

Sweet and Sour Sauce

You may use this one for cooking or dipping foods.

½ cup	pineapple juice
½ cup	white wine vinegar
2 tablespoons	peanut oil
2 tablespoons	packed light brown sugar
1 tablespoon	soy sauce
½ teaspoon	freshly ground black pepper
2 teaspoons	cornstarch mixed with
4 teaspoons	cold water

Mix first 6 ingredients in saucepan; bring to boil. Stir cornstarch mixture; add to hot mixture, stirring until sauce is clear and slightly thickened.
Yields 1½ cups.

High Voltage Mustard Sauce

Use sparingly. It's HOT.

3 tablespoons	dry mustard
2 tablespoons	peanut oil
2 tablespoons	water
¼ cup	sugar
1 tablespoon	cornstarch
½ teaspoon	salt
½ cup	water
¼ cup	white vinegar

Mix mustard and oil in small bowl. Gradually add 2 tablespoons water, stirring constantly, to form smooth paste. Stir together sugar, cornstarch and salt in wok: gradually add ½ cup water and vinegar. Blend thoroughly. Cook over medium heat, stirring constantly, until mixture thickens. Gradually add to mustard mixture, stirring constantly, until blended. Refrigerate until serving time. Stir before serving. Serve at room temperature.
Yields 1 cup.

Tempura Sauce

¼ cup	chicken stock
1 tablespoon	soy sauce
1 tablespoon	cream sherry
1 tablespoon	grated daikon*, optional
1 teaspoon	peeled and grated ginger root*

Combine first 3 ingredients. Just before serving, stir in daikon and ginger root.
Yields ½ cup.

"He-Man" Barbecue Sauce

2 tablespoons	vegetable oil
1	large onion, finely chopped
2 cloves	garlic, minced
1 cup	bottled chili sauce
½ cup	lemon juice
⅓ cup	molasses
3 tablespoons	Dijon mustard
1 tablespoon	Worcestershire sauce
¼ cup	dark rum

Heat oil in saucepan. Sauté onion and garlic until tender. Stir in chili sauce, lemon juice, molasses, mustard and Worcestershire. When this begins to boil, cover, lower heat and simmer 20 minutes. Stir often. Remove from heat and stir in rum.

At our house, my husband quadruples the recipe to make a half gallon plus 2 cups. The longer it keeps, the better it gets.
Yields 1¼ quarts.

Poi

Poi is a pale purplish-grey mush or paste made from the starchy staple tuber root called taro. Highly concentrated, it is an excellent staple food and balances the taste of the many zesty Island foods.

It has also been proclaimed to be one of the least allergenic foods a child can eat.

Ginger-Lime Dressing

4	lemons
4	limes
1 ounce	peeled and chopped ginger root*
¼ cup	honey
1 tablespoon	sugar
¼ cup	olive oil

In a small saucepan, combine the juice of lemons, juice of limes, ginger root, honey and sugar. Bring to a boil. Lower heat and simmer for 3 minutes, stirring occasionally. Cool and strain to remove chopped ginger. Add olive oil gradually, blending with wire whisk. *Yields 1 cup.*

Sidewalk Cafe Dressing

2 teaspoons	lemon juice
1 cup	red wine vinegar
1¼ tablespoons	salt
1 teaspoon	pepper, finely ground
1 tablespoon	Worcestershire sauce
1 teaspoon	Dijon mustard
1 clove	garlic, mashed
1 teaspoon	sugar
3 cups	corn oil

In blender, combine all ingredients except corn oil. Gradually add oil and blend again.
Yields 5 cups.

Ocean Dip

1 (8 ounce) package	cream cheese
1 (4½ ounce) can	shrimp, crabmeat or
	minced clam
1 tablespoon	milk
	or
1 heaping tablespoon	sour cream (enough to
	thin cream cheese)
1 heaping tablespoon	onion, chopped
1 tablespoon	horseradish
	salt and pepper to
	season

Mix all ingredients and bake at 300 degrees for 30 minutes, mixing once, until bubbly. Serve warm or cool.
Yields 1 cup.

Wiki Wiki Barbecue Sauce

1 cup	soy sauce
1 cup	ketchup
¼ cup	vinegar
¾ cup	sugar
¼ teaspoon	monosodium glutamate
1 piece	fresh ginger root*,
	peeled and mashed
¼ teaspoon	salt

In a medium size bowl, combine all the ingredients and mix until well blended. Makes a delicious marinating sauce for ribs or chicken.
Yields 3 cups.

Macadamia Lemon Butter

½ cup	butter
2 tablespoons	fresh lemon juice
	dash of pepper
½ cup	chopped Mauna Loa®
	macadamia nuts*
	or
½ cup	Bits O'Macadamia®*

In a small pan, heat butter until it foams, then brown slightly. Stir in lemon juice, pepper, and macadamias. Pour over hot cooked vegetables.
Makes topping for 6-8 vegetable servings.

NOTE: A quick way to "butter" hot cooked vegetables—spinach, green beans, asparagus, squash, peas, carrots, leeks, or celery. Especially good over vegetables with sieved hard-boiled eggs sprinkled over the top. Also use as a hot dressing to "wilt" lettuce for a superb salad: pour Macadamia Lemon Butter, while bubbling and hot, over broken leaf lettuce. Toss. Serve immediately.

Macadamia Nuts

This rich nut is true gourmet fare. Macadamia nuts are grown and packaged on the Big Island. They are delicious roasted, eaten plain or chocolate-covered. Most major grocery market chains on the Mainland carry the macadamia nut in cans or glass containers in the nut or specialty sections.

Chinese Sesame Dressing

6 tablespoons sesame oil*
2 tablespoons vinegar
1 teaspoon salt
2 teaspoons sugar
⅛ teaspoon monosodium glutamate

Combine ingredients in pint jar and shake well. Pour dressing over vegetable salad JUST BEFORE SERVING (to prevent wilting of greens).
Yields ½ cup.

Classy Plum Sauce

1 cup plum jam, jelly or
preserves
½ cup applesauce
½ teaspoon ground ginger
2 teaspoons cornstarch
2 teaspoons soy sauce
2 teaspoons wine vinegar

Mix plum jam and applesauce in saucepan; bring to a boil over medium heat. Combine ginger, cornstarch, soy sauce and vinegar; stir into jam mixture. Cook, stirring constantly, until mixture thickens. Cool. Refrigerate. Bring to room temperature before serving.
Yields 1 cup.

Hawaiian Harvest Stir-Fry

2 tablespoons	peanut oil
1	¼-inch slice fresh, peeled ginger root*
2 cups	small broccoli flowerets, blanched 3 minutes
2 cups	small cauliflowerets, blanched 3 minutes
1	green pepper, cored, seeded and cut in ¼-inch wide strips
2 cups	thin, diagonal celery slices
1	large clove garlic, peeled and minced
1 teaspoon	salt
1 teaspoon	freshly ground black pepper
2 tablespoons	soy sauce
½ cup	grated sharp Cheddar cheese

Heat oil in wok or skillet until hot. Add next five ingredients in order they are listed. Then add garlic, salt and pepper. Cover and cook about 10 minutes—just enough that vegetables are opaque. Add soy sauce; toss. Sprinkle grated cheese over vegetables. Let melt. Serve immediately.
Serves 6-8.

Yummy Yoga Yogurt In Pita Bread

This one is for the smart and sassy. It's not only delicious but loaded with nutrition.

1 cup	regular wheat germ
½ cup	plain yogurt
½ cup	cheese, grated
¼ cup	onion, finely chopped
¼ cup	green pepper, chopped
¼ cup	almonds, chopped
½ teaspoon	oregano, crushed
1 clove	garlic, minced
2 tablespoons	butter
2 tablespoons	oil
4	pita bread halves
	lettuce, shredded
	tomatoes, sliced
	olives, sliced
	green pepper, sliced
	alfalfa sprouts

Combine ¾ cup wheat germ, yogurt, cheese, onion, green pepper, almonds, oregano and garlic. Shape into small patties. Coat with remaining ¼ cup wheat germ. Heat butter and oil in skillet over medium heat. Brown patties. Place in pita bread with vegetables and mustard.
Serves 4.

Fried Ono Or Mahimahi

1 pound	fish
	salt and pepper
2	beaten eggs

1 cup   **crushed round crackers**
        oil for frying

Slice fish into one-half-inch thick pieces. Season with salt and pepper. Dip fish into beaten egg and then roll in crushed crackers. Fry in oil until browned.
Serves 2.

Surf Baked Beans

1 pound (2 cups)	**dry navy beans**
⅔ cup	**brown sugar**
2 quarts	**cold water**
½ teaspoon	**salt**
2 teaspoons	**dry mustard**
¼ cup	**molasses**
¼ pound	**salted pork**
1	**large onion, sliced**

Rinse beans. Add 2 quarts cold water to beans and bring to boil. Simmer 2 minutes, remove from heat and let stand 1 hour, covered. Add ½ teaspoon salt to beans that are soaking in water. Cover and simmer until tender (1 hour). Drain, reserving liquid. Measure 2 cups liquid, adding water if needed. Mix with sugar, mustard and molasses. Cut salted pork in half; score one half. Grind or thinly slice remainder. In a 2 quart bean pot or casserole, combine beans, onion, and ground salted pork. Pour sugar-bean liquid over ground pork. Top with scored salted pork. Cover and bake at 300 degrees 5 to 7 hours. Add more liquid if needed. For traditional New England Baked Beans, decrease brown sugar to ⅓ cup and increase molasses to ½ cup.
Serves 8.

Fluffy Gourmet Rice

¾ cup	white quick cooking rice
1½ cups	hot chicken broth or boullion
1 tablespoon	cooking oil
6	fresh green onions
⅓ cup	sliced fresh mushrooms
1	large tomato, peeled, seeded and chopped
3 tablespoons	chopped pimento
¾ teaspoon	salt (hold salt if using boullion)
¼ teaspoon	black pepper
2 tablespoons	slivered toasted almonds
2 tablespoons	sautéed raisins
	paprika

Cook rice as directed on box using broth or boullion for liquid. Heat oil in wok or large saucepan and add finely chopped onions, including green leafy tops. Cook until soft but not brown. Add mushrooms, rice, and tomato. Mix well. Add salt and pepper. Cover and heat 3 minutes. Turn off heat from wok or remove saucepan from stove. Toss rice mixture with fork and add pimento and raisins. Place a paper towel between lid and pan to absorb excess moisture. Add paprika and almonds when you are ready to serve.
Serves 6-8.

Baked Papaya

1	large firm ripe papaya*
1 tablespoon	butter
¾ teaspoon	salt
2 tablespoons	lemon juice

Pare and cut papaya lengthwise into six pieces. Remove the seeds. Sprinkle with salt, lemon juice and butter. Place in a baking pan, add enough water to cover bottom of pan to prevent burning and bake in a 350 degree oven for 35 minutes. Serve immediately. Serve in place of a vegetable.

Sunrise Omelet

3 slices	bacon
1 cup	chopped potatoes
4	eggs
1 teaspoon	parsley flakes
	dash of seasoned salt
	dash of onion powder
	dash of black pepper
1 tablespoon	butter
	cherry tomatoes
	or
	fresh parsley sprigs for
	garnish

Cook bacon until crisp, remove bacon, reserving drippings in skillet. Crumble bacon and set aside. Add potatoes to skillet; cook over medium heat until golden brown, stirring frequently. Remove from skillet and set aside. Combine eggs, parsley flakes, seasoned salt, onion powder and pepper; beat well. Melt butter in skillet; rotate pan to coat bottom. Pour egg mixture into skillet. As mixture starts to cook, gently lift edges of omelet with a spatula and tilt pan so the uncooked portion of egg will flow underneath. When done, serve warm and garnish with cherry tomato slices and parsley sprigs, if desired.
Serves 2-4.

Japanese Vegetables

2 tablespoons	peanut oil
1	small green pepper, cut in 1½-inch-long julienne strips
2	small carrots, pared, cut in 1½-inch-long julienne strips
½ rib	celery, cut in 1½-inch-long julienne strips
1	unpeeled zucchini, cut in 1½-inch-long julienne strips
2 tablespoons	chicken stock
1 (10 ounce) package	frozen snow peas*, thawed

Heat oil in wok or skillet. Add first two vegetables, stir 1 minute. Add second two vegetables; stir one minute. Add stock; cover; cook 30 seconds. Last, add snow peas; cook 1 minute. Season and serve immediately.
Serves 6.

Sweet Potatoes In Orange Basket

6	small oranges
2 cups	cooked sweet potatoes or yams, mashed
½ cup	sugar or ¾ cup brown sugar
2 tablespoons	butter, melted

¼ teaspoon   **cinnamon**
½ teaspoon   **ground ginger**
           dash of salt
1 teaspoon   **grated orange peel**
½ cup   **orange juice**
6   **marshmallows**

Cut oranges in half and scoop out pulp. In a saucepan combine sweet potatoes, sugar, butter, spices, salt, orange peel and orange juice. Cook for 15 minutes. Stuff oranges with sweet potato mixture and top each with a marshmallow. Place under broiler until marshmallows melt.
Serves 6.

Curried Avocado

4 tablespoons   **butter**
5 tablespoons   **flour**
2 cups   **milk**
1½ teaspoons   **salt**
½ teaspoon   **pepper**
2-3 teaspoons   **curry powder**
2 cups   **diced avocadoes**

Melt butter, add flour and stir to make a paste. Stir in milk gradually, cooking until the mixture thickens. Add curry powder, salt and pepper. Remove from heat. Add avocadoes just before serving. Serve with rice. Serve mango chutney, chopped macadamia nuts, shredded coconut, raisins or other condiments with this curry dish.
Serves 4.

Snow Peas Kahala Style

12 to 14	water chestnuts*, sliced ¼ inch thick
1 cup	thinly sliced fresh mushrooms
1 cup	diced onions
2 tablespoons	peanut oil
¾ pound	fresh snow peas*
	or
2 (6 ounce) packages	frozen snow peas*
1 teaspoon	salt
1 tablespoon	soy sauce
1 tablespoon	water
½ teaspoon	garlic powder

In a wok or large skillet with a tight fitting cover, sauté water chestnuts, mushrooms and onion in peanut oil for 5 minutes or until onion is tender. Add snow peas, salt, soy sauce and water. Mix well. Sprinkle with garlic salt. Cover tightly and simmer 5 minutes or until snow peas are tender but still crisp.
Serves 4-6.

Poi, Rice Or Bread?

Poi or rice is usually eaten in Island homes rather than bread. When bread is served, it is either sweet or exotic. Most Luaus I have attended offered the guests one or two of the many great breads found in this book.

Aloha Sweet Potatoes

4 to 5   medium sweet potatoes
½ cup   pineapple preserves
2 tablespoons   butter

Boil sweet potatoes in their peels until tender, about 25 minutes. Let cool, then peel and cut into ½ inch thick slices. In a large skillet, melt pineapple preserves and butter; add sweet potatoes. Cook gently, tossing lightly until sweet potatoes are glazed.
Serves 10-12.

Purple Cabbage
With Sweet-Sour Sauce

1   small onion, sliced
4 tablespoons   shortening
1 cup   grape juice
1   medium cabbage, sliced
thin
2   sour apples, sliced
2 tablespoons   salt
4 tablespoons   vinegar
2 tablespoons   brown sugar

Cook onion in shortening for 3 minutes. Add grape juice, cabbage, apples and salt. Cook until tender, about 30 minutes. Add vinegar and sugar and cook 5 minutes longer.
Serves 4-6.

Pao Doce
Portuguese Sweet Bread

1	**large potato**
2 tablespoons	**sugar**
1 package	**active dry yeast**
¼ cup	**milk**
1 teaspoon	**salt**
3	**large eggs**
¾ cup	**sugar**
¼ cup	**butter, melted**
4 cups	**flour**

Boil potato and save ¼ cup of the water in which it was boiled. Mash potato. Dissolve 2 tablespoons sugar and yeast into the potato water. Stir in mashed potato and allow to rise. Scald milk, add salt and allow to cool. Beat eggs in a large, warm mixing bowl and set aside 1 tablespoon of the beaten eggs. Slowly beat sugar and melted butter into beaten eggs. Combine egg and yeast mixtures. Add one-third of the flour and ¼ cup milk and beat well. Add another third of the flour and beat until blended. Put mixture onto a well-floured cutting board and add the rest of the flour. Knead well. Place in an oiled bowl and allow to rise twice its size. Punch down and divide into 2 well-greased loaf pans. Let rise again twice its size. Brush loaves with remaining egg mixture. Bake at 350 degrees for 35 to 45 minutes. Makes 2 loaves. *Serves 12-16.*

Orange Bread

3	oranges
2 quarts	water
2 teaspoons	salt
1½ cups	sugar
1 tablespoon	water
1 cup	sugar
2	eggs
1 cup	milk
2 tablespoons	butter, melted
3 cups	flour, sifted
½ teaspoon	salt
2 teaspoons	baking powder

Cut rind of three thick-skinned oranges into strips. Boil water and salt. Add orange rind and cook until tender. Blanch in cold water and drain. Boil rinds in sugar and 1 tablespoon water until syrup is absorbed. Watch rind closely and stir often to prevent burning as it scorches easily. Cool. Flour lightly. Cream 1 cup sugar, eggs, milk and butter. Sift together flour, salt and baking powder. Combine to make batter. Add orange rinds to batter. Turn batter into loaf pans. Bake at 350 degrees 30-45 minutes. Test with toothpick.
Makes 2 regular loaves or 3 small loaves.

Brown Walnut Bread

1 cup	flour
½ cup	sugar
2 teaspoons	baking soda
½ teaspoon	salt
1½ cups	graham flour
1½ cups	chopped walnuts
1 (6 ounce) can	evaporated milk
½ cup	water
1 tablespoon	vinegar
1	egg, beaten
1 cup	dark molasses
	maple syrup

Sift together flour, sugar, baking soda and salt into a large bowl. Stir in graham flour and 1 cup walnuts. Mix milk with water and stir in vinegar. Add to the flour mixture. Add egg and molasses to flour mixture and beat until well mixed. Place into a well-greased loaf pan and bake at 325 degrees for 1 hour and 15 minutes. Cool for 10 minutes. Remove from pan and allow to cool completely. Brush the top with maple syrup and sprinkle with remaining walnuts. Wrap in foil and store for at least 24 hours before serving.
Serves 6-8.

Sweet Potato Bread

2 packages	active dry yeast
¼ cup	warm water (105 degrees to 155 degrees)
1 cup	cooked sweet potatoes, mashed
1¾ cups	water
1½ teaspoons	salt
¼ cup	vegetable oil
1	egg
2 cups	whole wheat flour
4 cups	all-purpose flour
	butter or margarine, softened

Dissolve yeast in ¼ cup warm water in a large bowl. Stir sweet potatoes, water, salt, oil, and egg into dissolved yeast. Mix in flours. Turn dough onto lightly floured board. Knead until smooth and elastic, about 10 minutes. Place in greased bowl; turn greased side up and cover with towel. Let rise in warm place until double, about 50 minutes. Dough is ready if impression remains. Punch down dough; divide in half. Divide each half into thirds; shape into 6 rolls, 12 inches long. Braid 3 rolls carefully; repeat with remaining 3 rolls. Fold ends under loaves. Place seam side down on greased baking sheet. Let rise until double, about 40 minutes. Bake at 300 degrees 1 hour, or until done.
Serves 12.

Malasadas

Malasadas have long been a tasty pastry snack in Hawaii. They are very popular with all nationalities.

1 package	active dry yeast
1 teaspoon	sugar
¼ cup	warm water
6 cups	flour
½ cup	sugar
½ teaspoon	salt
¼ cup	melted butter
6	eggs
1 cup	evaporated milk
1 cup	softened butter
	vegetable oil for deep frying
	sugar and dash of nutmeg, mixed

Combine yeast with 1 teaspoon sugar; add warm water. Let stand for 5 minutes. Sift dry ingredients together in large bowl. Stir in melted butter. Beat eggs and milk together and add to flour mixture. Add yeast and mix well. Expect the dough to be sticky. Cover and let dough rise until doubled, punch it down. Let dough rise a second time. Heat oil in deep fryer to about 375 degrees. Dip finger tips in softened butter or cooking oil. Pinch off golf-ball sized pieces of raised dough. Drop in heated oil and cook until golden brown on one side. Turn over and fry until golden brown on other side. Drain on paper towels and roll in sugar-nutmeg mixture. Serve hot.
Makes 5 dozen.

Cheesy Macadamia Biscuits

These are elegant little biscuits. Great for family meals or large fanfares.

1½ cups	flour
½ teaspoon	salt
½ cup	soft butter
¼ pound	Swiss cheese, grated
1	egg
⅓ cup	chopped macadamia nuts*

Sift together flour and salt. Blend butter, cheese and egg. Slowly work in flour and nuts. Mold into a roll 1½ inches in diameter. Wrap in wax paper and chill until firm. Slice into ¼ inch sections. Place onto lightly buttered cookie sheets and bake at 400 degrees for 10 to 15 minutes. *Makes 3 dozen biscuits.*

Banana-Nut Bread

2 cups	flour
2½ teaspoons	baking powder
¼ teaspoon	baking soda
¼ teaspoon	salt
1 cup	mashed bananas
½ cup	butter
¾ cup	sugar
2	large eggs
½ cup	chopped unsalted macadamia nuts*

Sift together flour, baking powder, baking soda and salt. Mash bananas in a separate bowl. Add creamed butter and sugar and mix well. Mix in eggs and dry ingredients and fold in nuts. Pour into well-greased loaf pan and bake at 350 degrees for 50 minutes.
Serves 6-8.

Hawaiian Pineapple Mango Bread

2 cups	flour
1¼ cups	sugar
½ teaspoon	salt
2 teaspoons	cinnamon
2 teaspoons	baking soda
¾ cup	vegetable oil
3	eggs
1 (6 ounce) can	crushed pineapple
2 cups	diced mango*
½ cup	chopped nuts

Sift together all dry ingredients in a large mixing bowl. Mix well and add oil, eggs and pineapple. Beat well. Add mango and nuts. Pour into a well-greased and floured loaf pan and bake at 350 degrees for 40 minutes.
Serves 6-8.

Hawaiian Wedding Cake

I first ate this paradisiacal cake at our niece's graduation Luau in Honolulu. Her "Tutu" (grandmother) had made it and shared the recipe with us.

Mae

1 (18½ ounce) box	yellow cake mix
1 cup	pineapple juice
½ cup	mayonnaise
	Fluffy Delite Topping

Follow directions on box except using 1 cup juice from crushed pineapple in place of water. Add mayonnaise. Blend 4 minutes. Pour into a 9x13-inch pan. Bake at 350 degrees for 35 minutes or until toothpick comes out clean when inserted into center of cake. Cool cake completely before topping.
Serves 16.

Fluffy Delite Topping

1 (8 ounce) package	cream cheese, softened
1 (3 ounce) box	instant vanilla pudding
1 (20 ounce) can	crushed pineapple, drained (reserve liquid)
1 (8 ounce) container	nondairy whipped topping
½ cup	flaked coconut
½ cup	macadamia nuts*, chopped

Mix cream cheese and vanilla pudding and cream well. Fold in pineapple. Add ¼ of nondairy whipped topping and blend. Spread mixture on cooled cake. Top with remaining nondairy whipped topping. Sprinkle with coconut and nuts. Refrigerate until ready to serve.

Lehua Kahiapo
Kailua, Hawaii

Macadamia Nut Chocolate Soufflé

1 tablespoon	butter
1 (3½ ounce) jar	Bits O' Macadamia Nuts®*
4 tablespoons	sugar
3 tablespoons	flour
3	egg yolks
1½ cups	hot milk
4 ounces	semi-sweet chocolate, chopped
4	egg whites

Prepare a 1-quart soufflé dish by thoroughly buttering it, then sprinkle with ¼ cup of the macadamia nuts and 1 tablespoon of the sugar so it is completely covered. Combine remaining 3 tablespoons of the sugar, flour and egg yolks; beat until light yellow in color. Add hot milk slowly, beating continually. Cook in heavy saucepan until thick, stirring constantly. Remove from heat and add chocolate; stir until melted. Cool. Beat egg whites. Fold one fourth of the egg whites into the chocolate mixture to lighten it. Then fold in the remaining egg whites and the remaining macadamia nuts. Pour the soufflé mixture into the prepared dish. Place in oven preheated to 400 degrees, then immediately turn the oven down to 375 degrees. Bake for 25 to 30 minutes.
Serves 6.

Okinawa Sugar Cookies

3	eggs
½ teaspoon	vanilla
½ teaspoon	yellow coloring
1 cup	sugar
2 tablespoons	melted butter
3½ cups	flour
2 teaspoons	baking powder

Combine eggs, vanilla, coloring, sugar and butter. Sift flour and baking powder together. Add liquid. Mix dough well. Roll dough into strips of 2½-inch wide and ½-inch thick; cut crosswise into ¾ inch. Fry in deep fat. Cookies keep for weeks in air-tight container.
Makes 3 dozen.

Blossoms Of Love

The lei begins with an attitude, the attitude of Aloha. The full, fresh clusters of blossoms and buds, when laced together, form rare beauties. When you receive a lei in Hawaii, it is more than just a circle of sweet fragrant flowers given with a kiss. It is a spirit of thankfulness as each blossom is picked from the good earth and strung one at a time. It is a symbol of the wondrous Aloha spirit, made with care and given in a true spirit of love.

Often, thick spicy greenery is laced with the flowers. Nuts, berries, shells and an infinite variety of other items also go into the making of the lei.

The story goes that the lei-cum-kiss began in World War II when an entertainer dared to kiss an officer when presenting him with a lei. Embarrassed, she gave the excuse that it was a Hawaiian tradition. And so the lei greeting and kiss custom was born.

Macadamia Creme Chantilly

2 cups	milk
½ cup	sugar
1½ tablespoons	unflavored gelatin
½ teaspoon	salt
2	whole eggs
2	egg yolks
¼ cup	dark rum or 1½ teaspoons rum flavoring
1 cup	whipping cream
½ cup	Bits O' Macadamia Nuts®*
1 recipe	Macadamia Nut-Orange Sauce

Scald milk. Combine sugar, gelatin and salt. Beat whole eggs with egg yolks; add sugar mixture. Stir into hot milk. Set in top of double boiler and cook, stirring constantly, until mixture thickens slightly and coats spoon. Remove from heat and stir in rum. Chill until mixture begins to thicken, about the consistency of egg white. Whip cream. Fold in whipped cream and macadamia nuts. Chill a few minutes until mixture mounds when dropped from a spoon. Spoon into dessert dishes and chill 1 to 2 hours.
Serves 6-8.

Coconut Refrigerator Cake

4	egg yolks
2 cups	milk
2 tablespoons	flour
1 cup	sugar

                              pinch salt
          1 envelope   unflavored gelatin
                              dissolved in ½ cup
                              cold water
                    4   egg whites
                    1   small ready-made
                              chiffon cake
1 (8 ounce) carton   whipping cream
     2 tablespoons   sugar
        1 teaspoon   vanilla
               1 can   flaked coconut

Cook egg yolks, milk, flour, sugar and salt until spoon is coated. Remove the egg yolk mixture from heat and add gelatin. Cool. Beat egg whites and fold into pudding mixture. Tear cake by fistfuls. Place in 13x9-inch pan and pour custard over this. Whip cream, adding sugar and vanilla. Top with coconut.
Serves 10-12.

Tropical Champagne Compote

        1 cup   champagne
        1 cup   canned, seedless
                      lychees*, drained
        1 cup   cantaloupe balls
        1 cup   watermelon balls
        1 cup   tangerine slices
        1 cup   pineapple cubes, fresh
                      or canned, drained
        ¼ cup   Maraschino cherries
                      sprig of fresh mint

Pour champagne over fruit and let stand for about 20 minutes. Serve chilled in small cups. Garnish with sprig of mint.
Serves 6-8.

Aloha Fruitcake

1 cup	butter or margarine, softened
2 cups	sugar
5	eggs
3 cups	all-purpose flour
2 teaspoons	baking powder
¼ teaspoon	salt
1 cup	milk
1 cup	white raisins
1 cup	chopped walnuts
1 teaspoon	ground cinnamon
½ teaspoon	ground allspice
½ teaspoon	ground cloves
	Aloha Fruitcake Filling
	walnut halves (toasted)
	candied cherries

Cream butter, adding sugar gradually, beating well. Eggs should then be added one at a time, beating well after each one. Combine flour, baking powder and salt; add to creamed mixture alternately with milk, beginning and ending with dry mixture. Mix well after each addition. Stir in raisins and walnuts. Pour 2 cups plus 2 tablespoons batter into greased and floured 9-inch round pan; set aside. Stir cinnamon, allspice, and cloves into remaining batter; then pour into 2 greased and floured 9-inch round cake pans. Bake at 375 degrees for 25 minutes or until toothpick inserted into center comes out clean. Cool in pans 10 minutes; remove from pans and cool completely. Spread Aloha Fruitcake Filling between layers and on top of cake, stacking layers with *white* layer between the two spiced layers. Garnish top with toasted walnut halves and candied cherries.
Serves 10-12.

Aloha Fruitcake Filling

1 cup	sugar
1 tablespoon	all-purpose flour
1 cup	water
1½ cups	toasted flaked coconut
1 (8 ounce) can	crushed pineapple, undrained
2	oranges, peeled, sectioned, finely chopped

Combine sugar and flour in a small saucepan, mixing well; add water. Cook over medium heat 5 minutes, stirring occasionally. Add toasted coconut, pineapple and oranges. Cook 5 more minutes over medium heat. Cool mixture completely before spreading on cake.

Malihini (Newcomer) Haupia

⅓ cup	cornstarch
½ cup	sugar
⅛ teaspoon	salt
2 (12 ounce) cans	frozen coconut milk

Combine cornstarch, sugar, and salt. Add ½ cup of coconut milk and blend to smooth paste. Heat remaining milk and add cornstarch mixture. Cook for 20 minutes, stirring frequently until thickened. Pour into 8x8 inch pan. Cool and refrigerate. Cut into 1½ inch squares. Delicious anytime.
Serves 16-24.

Haupia Cake

10	egg whites
1 teaspoon	cream of tartar
½ cup	sugar
1½ cups	cake flour
3 teaspoons	baking powder
¾ cup	sugar
¼ teaspoon	salt
10	egg yolks
¼ cup	coconut milk or fresh milk
¼ cup	water
½ cup	oil
1 teaspoon	vanilla

Beat egg whites and cream of tartar until stiff but not dry. Gradually add sugar. Set aside. Sift dry ingredients together in a bowl. Make a well in dry ingredients. Add egg yolks, coconut milk, water, oil, and vanilla. Beat until smooth. Fold yolk mixture into beaten egg whites. Pour into ungreased 13x9 inch pan. Bake at 350 degrees 30 to 35 minutes. When cake is done turn pan upside down to cool about 45 minutes. Spread Haupia Frosting over cake.
Serves 12-16.

Haupia Frosting

1 (12 ounce) can	frozen coconut milk
2 cups	milk
½ cup	sugar
¼ teaspoon	salt
6 tablespoons	cornstarch
1½ teaspoons	vanilla
	fresh coconut, shredded

Combine all ingredients except shredded coconut. Cook coconut mixture over moderate heat, stirring constantly until thickened. Cool. Frost cake. Sprinkle with coconut.

Ono Honey Ambrosia

4	medium oranges, peeled and sliced crosswise
3	bananas, sliced crosswise
½ cup	orange juice
¼ cup	honey
2 tablespoons	lemon juice
¼ cup	flaked coconut
	Maraschino cherry halves

Combine fruit in a medium bowl. Combine orange juice, honey, and lemon juice. Pour over fruit, and mix well. Sprinkle with coconut; cover and chill at least an hour. Garnish with cherries. *Serves 6.*

Passion Fruit Chiffon Pie

1 tablespoon	plain gelatin
¼ cup	cold water
4	egg yolks, beaten until thick
½ cup	sugar
⅛ teaspoon	salt
½ cup	passion fruit* juice
4	egg whites, beaten stiff
½ cup	sugar

Dissolve gelatin in cold water and let stand. Cook over low heat egg yolks, sugar, salt, and juice, stirring until thickened. Add gelatin and mix well. Chill, stirring occasionally until ready to set. Beat egg whites and gradually add ½ cup sugar. Fold into egg yolk mixture. Pour into baked pie shell and chill for several hours.
Serves 6-8.

Coconut Puffs

2 cups	all-purpose flour
½ cup	sugar
3 teaspoons	baking powder
½ teaspoon	salt
¼ cup	vegetable oil
1 cup	coconut milk
2	eggs, beaten

Sift all dry ingredients together in a bowl and make a well. Then add vegetable oil, coconut milk and eggs. Mix thoroughly with spatula. Drop into deep hot oil by teaspoonfuls, frying for about 3 minutes or until golden brown. Drain on paper towels. These are delicious with coffee.

Makes about 3 dozen.

Fresh Pineapple Cobbler

4 cups	pineapple chunks
1 cup	sugar
⅓ cup	pancake mix
1 teaspoon	grated lemon peel
¾ cup	pancake mix
⅔ cup	sugar
1	beaten egg
¼ cup	butter

Combine first four ingredients and pour into a 9-inch-square pan. Combine next three ingredients and spread over pineapple mixture. Melt butter and drizzle over the top. Bake 35-40 minutes at 350 degrees. Serve warm with whipped cream or ice cream.

Serves 6-8.

Banana Spice Coffee Cake

2	extra-ripe, medium Dole® bananas, peeled
½ cup	packed brown sugar
1 teaspoon	ground cinnamon
¼ teaspoon	ground nutmeg
½ cup	butter
¾ cup	chopped walnuts
1 cup	all-purpose flour
1 cup	whole wheat flour
1 teaspoon	baking powder
1 teaspoon	baking soda
1 teaspoon	salt
½ cup	granulated sugar
3	eggs
1 teaspoon	vanilla extract
1 cup	raisins

Slice bananas into blender. Purée until smooth (1 cup). For topping, mix brown sugar, cinnamon and nutmeg. Cut in ¼ cup butter until mixture resembles coarse crumbs. Add walnuts. Combine flours, baking powder, baking soda and salt. Beat remaining ¼ cup butter with granulated sugar until light and fluffy. Beat in eggs and vanilla. Beat in flour mixture alternately with puréed bananas, ending with flour mixture. Stir in raisins. Spread half of batter in greased and floured 10 inch tube pan. Sprinkle with half of topping. Repeat layers once. Bake in 350 degree oven 45 to 50 minutes until cake tests done. Cool in pan, then turn onto plate.
Serves 12.

Volcano Watermelon

Cut one end of the watermelon so it can sit flat. Do not cut through rind. Carve the other end with your pattern to form an opening. Use as an unusual punch bowl after cleaning out the meat or leave half of the meat in and finish heaping full with cantaloupe, honeydew melon, and watermelon fruit balls. Add strawberries and blackberries for contrast and more flavor. If you like, sit melon on tray and place fruit around bottom. A lovely and unusual conversation piece.

Honey Of A Honeydew

    1   **honeydew melon**
        assorted fruits

Cut the honeydew in half, carving the edges in a zig zag pattern. Scoop out melon, toss in combination of scooped cantaloupe, papayas, pineapple, bananas (dipped in citrus juice to preserve color), strawberries and blueberries.
Serves 2.

Haupia
(Coconut Pudding)

This is the real Kamaaina (old-timers') way to make Haupia. Always served at Luaus. Delicious anytime.

6 cups	grated coconut (2 coconuts)
3 tablespoons	cornstarch for *soft* pudding, or
6 tablespoons	cornstarch for *firm* pudding
2 cups	boiling water
3½ tablespoons	sugar

Pour boiling water over coconut and allow to stand for 15 minutes. Strain through double thickness of cheesecloth, squeezing out just as much of the milk as possible, about 3 cups. Mix cornstarch with sugar and add sufficient coconut milk to make a smooth paste. Heat remaining milk to boiling and slowly stir in cornstarch paste. Boil until it thickens. Pour into mold and allow to cool. Cut into squares and serve on squares of ti leaves, if available. If not, serve on bamboo plates or glass platters.
Serves 16-24.

Ice Cream Da Pineapple Way

Mmm ono ono (good good)!

3	small pineapples
½ gallon	pineapple ice cream

> **1 cup   freshly grated coconut**
> **½ cup   slivered almonds**

Twist crown of pineapple to left and it will fall off. Cut pineapple in half. Core out center, preserving the shell. Scoop ice cream into each shell along with coconut and almond. Keep in freezer until ready to serve.

You may freeze pineapple meat or use in another dish. Root your pineapple crown by following the directions given in this book. *Serves 6.*

Yak-Kwa
(Korean Holiday Cookies)

> **1 cup   sugar**
> **¼ cup   water**
> **½ cup   honey**
> **2½ cups   sifted flour**
> **¼ cup   oil**
> **¼ cup   whiskey**
> **¼ cup   finely chopped almonds**

Heat sugar with water until sugar dissolves. Add honey and stir until completely mixed. Put flour in a large mixing bowl. Add oil, whiskey and ¼ cup of the warm sugar mixture. Mix thoroughly. The texture should be similar to pie crust dough. Roll dough to ¼ inch thick. Cut into 1 inch squares or triangles. Fry in deep hot oil until brown. Drain on paper towels. While cookies are still warm, soak in the remaining sugar syrup for 2 to 3 minutes each. Roll in finely chopped nuts. Cool. *Makes 2-3 dozen.*

Frozen Heaven

12	marshmallows
¼ cup	pineapple juice
1 cup	heavy cream, whipped
½ cup	orange sections
1 cup	crushed pineapple, drained
2	bananas, mashed
1 tablespoon	lemon juice
½ cup	Maraschino cherries
¼ cup	chopped nuts
¾ cup	macaroon crumbs

Cut marshmallows into small pieces. Heat them in pineapple juice until marshmallows dissolve. Remove from heat and beat until cool. Add whipped cream and beat again. Fold in well-drained orange sections, pineapple, banana pulp mixed with lemon juice, cherries, nuts and macaroon crumbs. Turn into refrigerator tray and freeze without stirring.
Serves 8-10.

Coconut Mousse

1 pint	half-and-half
3 (¼ ounce) packages	unflavored gelatin
⅓ cup	water
1 cup	sugar
2 cups	grated moist coconut
1½ pints	whipping cream
1 teaspoon	coconut extract

Bring half-and-half just to a boil in a saucepan. Dissolve gelatin in water. Add gelatin mixture and sugar to half-and-half, continue cooking until sugar dissolves. Cool and add coconut. Beat coconut extract and cream until stiff. Fold in whipped cream and pour into an 8 cup mold. Chill until firm.
Serves 10.

Coconut Upside Down Cake

½ cup	butter or margarine
1 cup	brown sugar
1½ cups	shredded coconut
¼ cup	shortening
¾ cup	sugar
1	egg
1¼ cups	sifted flour
2 teaspoons	baking powder
¼ teaspoon	salt
½ cup	milk
½ teaspoon	vanilla

Melt butter and sugar together in the bottom of an 8x8x2 inch pan. Sprinkle coconut over bottom. Cream shortening and add sugar gradually. Add egg and beat well. Sift together dry ingredients and add them alternately with milk to sugar mixture. Add vanilla. Pour batter over the coconut mixture. Bake in a 350 degree oven until done, about 40 minutes.
Serves 6-8.

Hawaiian Chess Pie

You may use walnut bits in place of macadamia nut bits.

1 cup	raisins
½ cup	butter, melted
3	eggs, beaten
1 cup	sugar
1 (8¼ ounce) can	crushed pineapple, drained
½ cup	macadamia nut* bits
½ teaspoon	vanilla
1	unbaked pie shell

Soak raisins in hot water until double in size. Drain well and pat dry. Combine butter, eggs, and sugar; beat well. Add raisins, pineapple, nuts, and vanilla. Pour into pie shell and bake in 400 degree oven for 10 minutes. Lower heat to 350 degrees for 30 minutes. Bake until knife inserted comes out clean.
Serves 6-8.

Chinese Almond Cookies

1 cup	cake flour
¾ cup	powdered sugar
¼ teaspoon	salt
½ cup	finely ground, blanched almonds
6 tablespoons	peanut oil
1	well-beaten egg
1 teaspoon	almond extract
	whole blanched almonds

Sift together the dry ingredients, including ground almonds. Add peanut oil. Stir in the egg and extract. Roll out about ¼ inch thick. Cut into small rounds. Press a whole blanched almond in the center of each. Bake in a 375 degree oven for 15 minutes.
Makes 2 dozen.

Macadamia Orange Cheesecake-Pie

1¼ cups	graham cracker crumbs
1 cup	sugar, divided
¼ cup	butter or margarine, melted
⅔ cup	Mauna Loa® macadamia nuts*, divided
4 (3 ounce) packages	cream cheese, softened
2	eggs, lightly beaten
1 teaspoon	grated orange peel

Preheat oven to 350 degrees. In a small bowl combine graham cracker crumbs, ¼ cup of the sugar and butter. With the back of a spoon, press onto bottom and sides (not on rim) of a 9-inch pie pan. Refrigerate while preparing filling. Chop ½ cup of the macadamia nuts; set aside. In a medium bowl combine cream cheese, eggs, orange peel and remaining ¾ cup sugar. Beat until smooth. Fold in chopped macadamia nuts. Pour into prepared crust. Sprinkle with remaining macadamia nuts cut in halves. Bake until firm, about 30 minutes. Let cool completely on wire rack. Serve at room temperature.
Serves 8.

Pineapple Ice

1 cup	sugar
⅔ cup	water
1	fresh pineapple
⅓ cup	fresh lime juice
1	large egg white

Mix sugar and water together in a saucepan over low to medium heat; stir frequently until sugar dissolves and syrup starts to simmer. Chill. Cut pineapple in half lengthwise, leaving crown intact. Carve fruit from pineapple, leaving ½-inch of fruit in the rind. Remove core and slice fruit into 1-inch chunks. Place pineapple halves in large tightly sealed plastic bags and freeze until ready to use. In a food processor (with lower blade intact), add pineapple chunks and process until fruit is smooth and well puréed. There should be about 2 cups purée. Add chilled syrup and juice from lime. Process 10 seconds. Place mixture in tray or bowl and partially freeze. With lower metal blade in place, place spoonfuls of partially frozen pineapple mixture in bowl of processor. Mix by turning processor on and off about 6 times, then process about 2 minutes until completely blended, smooth and fluffy. With machine running, add egg white through feed slot. Run 1 more minute. Refreeze. Spoon into pineapple shells and serve.
Serves 6.

Passion Fruit Cookies

½ cup	margarine
1 cup	sugar
1	egg
4 tablespoons	passion fruit* juice
	(fresh, if possible)
1¼ cups	flour

2 teaspoons	baking soda
½ teaspoon	salt
1 cup	cornflakes
1 cup	rolled oats
½ cup	nuts, chopped
½ cup	dates or figs, sliced thin

Cream margarine, sugar, and eggs. Add passion fruit juice and mix well. Sift flour, baking soda, and salt and add to the creamed mixture. Add oats, nuts, dates, and cornflakes; mix well. Grease pan, drop by teaspoonfuls and bake at 375 degrees for 12 minutes.
Makes 3-4 dozen.

Macadamia Ice Cream Dessert

1 package	plain chocolate wafers, crushed (about 1¼ cups crumbs)
¼ pound	melted butter
½ gallon	chocolate ice cream
1½ cups	chopped Mauna Loa® macadamia nuts* or 1½ cups Bits O' Macadamia®

Combine chocolate crumbs with butter and mix thoroughly. Press into a 9x13x2 inch cake pan. Cut ice cream into about 1½ inch thick slices and lay the slices close together over the crust, blending them together with a knife as the ice cream melts slightly until it is spread evenly over the entire pan. Top with nuts and freeze until needed.
Serves 16-18.

Peach Ginger Coffee Cake

1 (16 ounce) can	peach slices
⅓ cup	packed light brown sugar
1½ cups	all-purpose flour
¼ teaspoon	baking soda
½ teaspoon	cinnamon
½ teaspoon	ground ginger
¼ teaspoon	ground cloves
¼ teaspoon	salt
½ cup	light molasses
½ cup	boiling water
¼ cup	salad oil
1	egg

Grease and flour one 8x8 pan. Drain peach slices well; pat dry with paper towels and arrange in bottom of baking pan. Sprinkle brown sugar over peach slices. In large bowl, with fork, mix flour and next 6 ingredients; add remaining ingredients and stir just until blended. Carefully pour batter over peach slices and bake in a 350 degree oven for 30 to 35 minutes. Cool cake in pan on wire rack 10 minutes. With knife, loosen cake from pan and invert onto plate.
Serves 6-8.

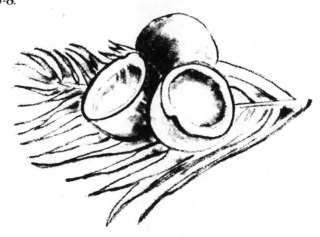

Food And Flowers
Go Together In Paradise

In Hawaii, flowers take their rightful place—from adorning a simple breakfast plate to enhancing the most elegant affair.

Fragrant blossoms are picked daily from the powdery brown earth and used lavishly as table decorations and food garnishes. Guests adorn themselves for mealtime with flowers in their hair, and garlands around their necks, wrists or ankles.

The extravaganza of flowers compliments the freshly homegrown fruits and vegetables in Hawaii.

Each island even claims its very own special flower as shown throughout **Hawaiian Magic.**

Orange Pound Cake

1 cup	margarine
2 cups	sugar
5	eggs
3 cups	sifted flour
3 teaspoons	baking powder
¼ teaspoon	salt
¾ cup	orange juice (must be fresh, not frozen)
	grated rind of 1 orange
¼ cup	margarine
⅓ cup	bourbon
⅔ cup	sugar

Cream margarine and sugar until fluffy. Beat in eggs one at a time. Sift dry ingredients and add to batter alternately with orange juice, ending with orange juice. Add grated rind. Pour into a greased and floured tube pan. Bake at 350 degrees for 1 hour. Remove cake from the oven, put the margarine, bourbon and sugar in a saucepan and heat until the sugar is dissolved. This will be the glaze. DO NOT LET BOIL. Prick the top of the cake with a fork and then pour glaze evenly over the cake. Leave in the pan until thoroughly cooled. This cake can be made ahead and frozen, or kept in the refrigerator until ready to serve. *Serves 10.*

Tahitian Ice Cream Cake

12	lady fingers, split lengthwise
1 (8 ounce) can	crushed pineapple or chopped mangoes*
1 pint	vanilla ice cream, softened

Line bottom of 8x8 inch square pan with lady fingers and spread the ice cream on top. Top with pineapple or mangoes. Cut in squares and serve immediately.
Serves 6.

Ginger Dreams

1 cup	sugar
1 cup	warm water
4½ cups	sifted flour
1 tablespoon	ground ginger
3 level teaspoons	baking soda
1 teaspoon	cinnamon
½ teaspoon	salt
	a little less than a cup of melted shortening
1 cup	light molasses

Mix all ingredients together. Bake a few minutes in a 375 degree oven and then turn down oven to 350 degrees. Bake until cookies spring back when tested by pressing lightly with a finger. Frost with the following:

Grate rind and juice of ½ of a medium orange. Mix with enough powdered sugar and water to make a thick frosting. Place a dab on each hot cookie when they come out of the oven. The frosting will spread over each cookie as it melts.
Makes 2 dozen.

Hawaiian Fruit Cake

1½ cups	raisins
1 cup	golden raisins
1½ cups	candied orange peels, chopped
1½ cups	candied lemon peels, chopped
1½ cups	red glazed Maraschino cherries, halved
1 tablespoon	candied ginger, chopped
1 (20 ounce) can	crushed pineapple, drained
2 cups	coconut, shredded
1½ cups	citron, chopped
¼ cup	brandy
¼ cup	honey
¼ cup	butter, melted
½ cup	guava* jam
8	eggs, beaten
2⅔ cups	flour, sifted
2 teaspoons	cinnamon
2 teaspoons	allspice
2 teaspoons	nutmeg
1½ teaspoons	baking powder
½ teaspoon	salt
1 teaspoon	baking soda
1½ cups	macadamia nuts*, chopped
1½ cups	butter
1 cup	brown sugar
½ cup	macadamia nuts*, chopped

Combine fruits with brandy, honey, butter, jam, and eggs, mixing well. Allow to set overnight. Combine flour, cinnamon, allspice, nutmeg, baking powder, salt, baking soda, and 1½ cups nuts. Cream together butter and brown sugar. Add dry ingredients. Stir batter into fruit mixture. Line 3 (5x9-inch) loaf pans with foil. Pour batter into pans, and sprinkle tops with ½ cup macadamia nuts. Bake in a 275 degree oven for 15 minutes, and then at 250 degrees for 1 hour and 45 minutes, until toothpick comes out clean.
Makes 3 loaves.

Mango Pie

1¼ cups	wheat flour, sifted
¾ teaspoon	salt
1 teaspoon	baking soda
½ cup	shortening
¼ cup	milk
4 cups	mango*, sliced
2 tablespoons	minute tapioca
½ cup	honey
1 tablespoon	lemon juice
½ teaspoon	ground cinnamon
¼ teaspoon	allspice

To make pie crust, combine flour, salt, and baking soda. Cut in shortening. Add milk, slowly mixing with fork. Roll out dough and line a pie pan. Set aside.

For filling, combine mango, tapioca, honey, lemon juice, cinnamon and allspice. Fill pie shell and bake at 425 degrees for 10 minutes. Lower heat to 350 degrees and bake 30 more minutes. If mango is unavailable, substitute 5 to 6 cups of sliced green apples. Increase honey to ¾ cup and omit lemon juice.
Serves 6-8.

Macadamia Lime Chiffon Pie

This one is terrific.

½ cup	sweetened flaked coconut
1	unbaked pastry pie shell (8-inch homemade or 9-inch frozen and thawed)
1 envelope	unflavored gelatin
⅓ cup	fresh lime juice
4	eggs, separated
1 cup	sugar, divided
½ cup	water
2 tablespoons	rum
⅔ cup	chopped macadamia nuts*, divided
	whipped cream

Sprinkle coconut evenly over the bottom and side of pie shell, pressing firmly with the back of a spoon so coconut adheres. Prick bottom and side of pastry with fork tines. Refrigerate until firm, about 1 hour. Preheat oven to 425 degrees. Bake pie shell until golden, about 10 minutes, pricking crust occasionally with fork tines if bubbling occurs. Remove from oven; set aside until cooled. In a small bowl combine gelatin and lime juice; set aside to soften. In a medium saucepan beat egg yolks with a wire whisk; add ½ cup of the sugar and water. Cook and stir over low heat until thickened, about 5 minutes (do not boil). Stir reserved gelatin mixture into the hot liquid; remove from heat. Spoon into a large bowl; cover with plastic wrap and cool to room temperature. Stir in rum and ½ cup sugar; beat until stiff (but not dry) peaks form. Fold egg whites into yolk mixture. Pour into reserved cooled pie shell.
Serves 8.

Magic After Dark—The Luau

A Hawaiian party is a great way to celebrate a special occasion in the lives of friends or loved ones. Graduations, weddings, birthdays, and promotions are all events which can be made even more special when you create a little bit of paradise for your guests. This graceful and colorful form of entertainment can be adapted to any setting—an apartment, large home, backyard, or poolside. Let your imagination go and have the time of your life!

The success of a Luau, whether large or small, comes from the heart and effort of the host and hostess. Good planning, of course, is the prerequisite to all going well. Then the ones doing the entertaining can relax and enjoy themselves with their guests.

Of course, the start of any party is preparing the guest list. The number of guests you invite is limited only by the size of the location. Invitations should highlight your Hawaiian theme, perhaps by using brightly colored paper or tropical illustrations for the invitations. One great idea is to use your menu title as your party theme on invitations, such as "Tiki Tiki Waikiki". Good examples are surf scenes, palm tree and moon, or hula dancers. Let your guests know that they should dress casually, wearing brightly colored Hawaiian prints. The colorfully attired guests add even more zest to your decor.

The object of a Luau is to have fun, so choose foods which are simple to prepare or can be prepared ahead of time. We have chosen several suggested menus which can help you decide. They range from the traditional Hawaiian Luau, complete with imu, to simpler menus for modern lifestyles. Traditional Hawaiian food is not necessary, but try to include some dishes typical of the Islands. A Luau is perfect for pot luck, too. Ask each guest to prepare a recipe you have selected.

Your centerpiece can also be part of your menu. Pineapples, watermelons and other fruits make attractive, edible decorations.

Your Luau should have an attractive tropical look to carry out your Hawaiian theme. Use as much greenery as you can round up. Ferns, palms, ficus or local greenery add a lush look. Orchids or local blossoms in season are beautiful as table decorations, floated in water, or pinned in the ladies' hair. Hawaiian Luaus have bits of greenery such as fern fronds or ti leaves sprinkled all over the table with a flower by each place setting. Tiki torches and candles add to the exotic mood. Tiki torches may be purchased or rented. It has been our experience that kerosene is a better fuel than the more expensive tiki torch fuel. If properly prepared, you should have hours of flickering flames. Be sure to soak the wicks well in the fuel before immersing in the fuel container. Light about an hour in advance to burn off excess kerosene residue. Scented candles also add to your party decor. They can be located in the pool or in large bowls of water as centerpieces. Some people like to put the candles in frisbees when floating them in the swimming pool so they will burn longer. You may also wish to turn off the pool pump so the candles will float freely on the surface and not be drawn to the edge. A nice touch in your powder room is to float candles in the bathtub and shut the glass shower door for a lovely diffused glow.

For seating, tables and chairs can be used, or straw mats placed on the ground. Large floor pillows make comfortable, casual seating inside. Hawaiians help themselves to the floor for genuine comfort. Buffet style service saves wear and tear on the hostess, and allows the guests to help themselves. Cover the tables with long strips of butcher paper to cover table tops, and use colorful paper plates, cups, and disposable utensils. After the Luau, you can simply remove the items you wish to keep, roll up the butcher paper, and toss away.

Luau entertainment depends on your location and budget. Hawaiian music is an integral part of the Luau. Use live musicians if at all possible, or play tapes and records of Hawaiian melodies. Hula dancers always add authenticity to a Luau. Often, they can be hired through local dancing schools at nominal cost. Audience participation is fun, too! Many family Luaus in Hawaii begin in the late afternoon so guests can play volleyball or take a dip in the pool before dark. Hawaiians love games, so by all means, have board games and cards ready for after dinner. Other ideas are prizes for the most authentically dressed, an amateur band for musical guests, or a hula contest.

Not to be overlooked is cooperation from Mother Nature, especially if your event is to be held outdoors. A gentle, soft evening certainly enhances a Luau. Check the calendar for a half to full moon, if possible. Set up an alternate location indoors or rent a tent if the weather looks unpredictable.

These suggestions, plus your own creativity, will help you create a little corner of Hawaii no matter where you live.

Over Which Ear
Do I Wear My Flower?

It is Hawaiian tradition for ladies to wear flowers in their hair. The placement of your flower can tell the men where they stand in matters of romance.

If a lady is taken, she wears her flower over her left ear, on the side where her heart is. She wears her flower on the right side if available.

A "wise wag" once told me that if a woman is taken but still looking, or if she has simply run out of luck, the flower goes on top of her head. The truth of this remains to be seen!

How To Prepare An Imu
Hawaiian Underground Oven

In preparing an imu, as we Hawaiians say, all the items below are required:

1. Kindling wood.
2. Kerosene.
3. Porous lava rocks of various sizes.
4. Firewood split in halves or quarters.
5. Eight banana stumps cut into two-foot sections, mashed, and shredded.
6. Banana and ti leaves.
7. Twelve burlap sacks cut open to full size.
8. Two large canvas tarps.
9. Two large non-galvanized sheets of chicken wire, each six feet by six feet.
10. Non-galvanized tie wire eight feet long.
11. One long-handled tong.
12. Work bench
13. Hawaiian rock salt.
14. Two large pans.
15. One two inch by seven foot pipe.

Select a soft ground site where digging won't be difficult. The diameter and depth of the imu, as well as the cooking time, depend on the size and weight of the fully cleaned and dressed pig. A fifty pound pig would take approximately two and a half to three hours of cooking in a hole five feet in diameter and gradually tapered to three feet deep.

After the hole is dug, place pipe vertically in the center of the hole. It should extend well above the rim of the hole. Lay kindling wood on the bottom around the pipe and wet with kerosene. Fill the hole with firewood, stacking crisscross around the pipe and up to the rim of the hole. Next, pile lava rocks on wood, building a pile like a pyramid. Remove pipe from hole, wet a piece of burlap with kerosene, light and push down into the center of the hole. Let fire burn approximately two hours or until all wood is burned and rocks are red hot. When rocks settle in hole, remove all unburned wood and level rocks around hole. Hint . . . prepare your rock oven and have it ready to fire up the day before you actually cook your pig. Cover imu with canvas and light the fire when preparing the pig.

To prepare the pig for roasting, the pig must be completely cleaned and dressed. Cut pig between both front legs and rib cage to make pocket cavities. Sit pig on a large sheet of chicken wire. Sprinkle Hawaiian rock salt into open cavities and abdomen areas. Stuff small red hot rocks in abdomen and foreleg cavities. Tie all four legs together with tie wire, completely wrap chicken wire around pig and tie together.

With rocks red hot and the pig ready for cooking, line hole with shredded banana stumps, banana and ti leaves. Lay pig in center of hole with back on bottom. Additional foods can be cooked with the pig, such as sweet potatoes, poultry, fish, and wild game. Place another large sheet of chicken wire over the pig and all other foods. Cover pig and food with lots of banana and ti leaves. Cover over everything with burlap bags pre-soaked in water, making sure bags overlap rim of hole about one foot. Completely cover hole with the rest of burlap bags overlapping each other, and with two large canvas tarps. Finally cover hole with dirt, starting at base. Slightly wet dirt with water and keep watch on imu for any steam leaks. If leaks occur, cover with more dirt.

After cooking time is over, carefully remove dirt off canvas by scraping it away with shovel. Carefully lay back each canvas tarp from top to base. Then carefully remove each burlap bag in the same way. Finally remove top sheet of chicken wire, banana and ti leaves.

Description Of Illustrations

Figure 1:   Five feet in diameter by three feet deep.

Figure 2:   Two inch pipe placed in hole.

Figure 3:   Kindling wood in bottom of hole around pipe.

Figure 4:   Firewood over kindling to rim of hole.

Figure 5:   Remove pipe after lava rocks are piled over firewood.
Wrap one-half burlap bag on end of pipe. Presoak in
kerosene. Light burlap and push into pipe hole to kindling wood to start fire.

Figure 6:   Rocks settle in hole after all wood in burned. Remove
all unburned wood and level rocks.

Figure 7:   Lay shredded banana stumps, banana and ti leaves on
rocks.

Figure 8:   Center pig in hole; add other food to be cooked.
Cover hole with second sheet of chicken wire. Cover
with more banana and ti leaves, then burlap, canvas,
and finally, dirt.

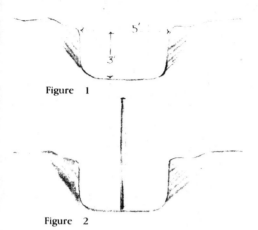

Figure 1

Figure 2

Figure 6

Figure 3

Figure 7

Figure 4

Figure 8

Figure 5

Kamaaina (Old Timer) Luau Menu

Kalua Pig
Lomi Lomi Salmon
Pipikaula
Sweet Potatoes
Opihi
Fresh Pineapple
Assorted Cakes and Variety
   Drinks

Aku (Raw Fish)
Green Onions with Hawaiian
   Rock Salt
Chicken Long Rice
Steamed Fish
Poi
Haupia
Banana Bread

In Hawaii, a Luau is an O'hana (family or clan) occasion. Everyone pitches in to help prepare for the celebration. Some provide the live music, others prepare the imu (underground oven), still others assemble the temporary shelter made of a frame covered with canvas on the top and palm leaves on the sides. Carrying out all the preparations is done in a spirit of love and lots of fun.

A Luau can be for an immediate family of a dozen or so, or up to hundreds of relatives . . . children, cousins, aunties, uncles, tutus and tutukanes (grandmas and grandpas) and friends.

On the day of the Luau, music, fun and dancing goes on all day long and into the evening, amidst a bountiful supply of fresh flowers and favorite Island foods.

One of the most frequently asked questions on the Mainland is, "How do you cook the pig under the ground in Hawaii?" The answer is, "In an imu."

FRESH CUTTING IDEAS

QUARTERS: (1) Divide the pineapple in half and then quarters, cutting from the bottom through the crown with a sharp knife. (2) Cut out the hard, fibrous core. Leave the crown on for decoration. (3) Loosen fruit by cutting close to the rind. Use a sharp, straight knife or a curved, serrated one. (See information about the pineapple knife below.) (4) Cut crosswise through the fruit several times, then lengthwise once or twice to make pieces bite-size.

PINEAPPLE RUBY: (1) With a sharp knife, cut off top and bottom of pineapple. Save the top and crown. (2) Insert knife close to rind, and cut completely around the pineapple with a sawing motion. (3) Remove the cylinder of pineapple and cut into spears. Put spears back together to form the cylinder again. (4) Set the rind on the serving dish, and put the cylinder of spears back inside. Put the top back on the pineapple so that it looks uncut.

OUTRIGGER: (1) Quarter the pineapple, leaving the crown on. (2) Loosen fruit by cutting under and around the core, but without removing the core. Then insert knife close to rind and loosen fruit from rind. (3) Remove the fruit and cut crosswise several times. (4) Slip sections of fruit back into the shell under the core and arrange in a staggered pattern.

SPEARS: (1) With a sharp knife, cut off the top and bottom of the pineapple. Then, doing a strip at a time, cut the rind away. (2) Remove the "eyes" by cutting away diagonal strips. (3) Cut cylinder of fruit into spears. To make smaller wedges, cut spears crosswise.

A pineapple knife may be purchased from a gourmet shop or department store.

Dole®

QUARTERS

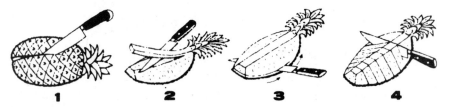

PINEAPPLE RUBY

OUTRIGGER

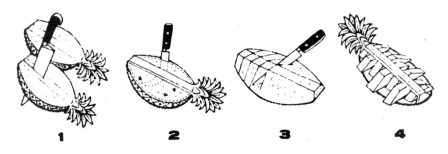

SPEARS

Dole®

HOW TO GROW YOUR OWN PINEAPPLE

IT'S EASY TO GROW your own pineapple, regardless of where you live. Start with a fresh pineapple. The crown (the top leafy part) is what you need to save for planting. Remove it from the pineapple by simply twisting it off; trim away any of the fruit that may still be stuck to the crown.

Strip away a few of the lower leaves. Find a dry, shady spot and place the crown upside down there for about a week to allow the cut end and leaf scars to harden (to prevent rot).

HOW TO PLANT

When you're ready to plant the crown, start with an eight-inch porous red clay pot. As the plant grows, transplant it to a larger, 12-inch pot.

Good drainage is important. In the bottom of the pot, place broken chunks of an old pot covered with up to an inch of coarse gravel. Then add the soil. Use a good light garden soil, mixed with up to one-third well-composted organic matter.

Place the crown in the soil and firmly press down the soil around the base of the crown. Avoid getting any soil into the leaves.

USEFUL GROWING TIPS

▶Fertilize your pineapple when you plant it and every two or three months. Use a good household plant food, and follow the label directions for amount to use and how to use it.

▶Pineapples need water, but not very often. Wetting the soil once a week should be sufficient.   Dole®

▶ Pineapples are tropical plants. If you live in a year'round warm climate, your pineapple should do well in your garden. If your climate gets cold, keep your plant indoors during cold seasons as frost or freezing temperatures will kill it. In warm seasons, keep it on a sunny porch or in the garden.

▶When keeping your pineapple indoors, place it near a window during the day where it will get lots of sunlight. Move it away from the window at night to prevent chilling.

▶When keeping your pineapple indoors, place it near a window during the day where it will get lots of sunlight. Move it away from the window at night to prevent chilling.

▶In a way, pineapples can get sunburned, too, after spending a winter indoors. When moving your plant outdoors for the summer, keep it in a semi-shaded spot for a few days.

WAITING FOR THE FRUITS OF YOUR LABOR

Don't expect a harvest the first year! In Hawaii, it takes a crown about two years to produce a ripe fruit, so expect to wait at least that long for your own.

In the meantime, it's interesting to watch the plant develop. When the plant is about a year and a half old, you should be able to see a bright red cone that grew out of a bud formed in the center of the leaves. If it hasn't appeared by the twentieth month, pineapple experts suggest that you "remind" the plant of "its responsibility." Put the pineapple (pot and all) and a good, red apple in a solid plastic bag, tightly tie it closed, and leave it in a shady spot for three days. Then open the bag and return the plant to its usual sunny spot. The bright red cone should appear in two months!

This cone, or bud, grows up above the leaves. When it is two or three inches long, rows of long, tiny bluish flowers will begin to appear, starting around the base. Each flower blooms for only one day, and the flowering is complete within two weeks. As each flower dries, it leaves an "eye." At first the eyes of a pineapple are pointed, but as the fruit ripens, they smooth out.

As the fruit develops, it gradually becomes sweeter. Inside, the flesh changes from white to yellow. Outside, the shell changes from green to a rich golden color. When the fruit is golden halfway up, the pineapple is finally ready to be picked! Dole®

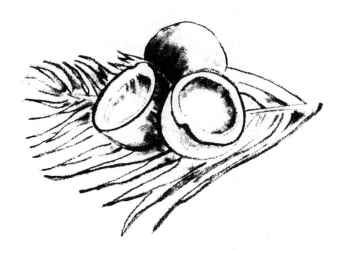

Coconut (Niu)

The coconut is the largest nut in the world, and provides a very distinctive sweet, natural flavor. Until recently, this brown tropical nut remained an aggravating mystery to me.

This past summer, we were in Waialua, Oahu at Lee's Dad's home. I asked "Grandpa" if he would show me how to crack and shell a coconut. He picked one from the tree in the front yard. First he removed the husk. With easy skill, he rotated the nut in his hands as he tapped around the middle with a hammer. And "voila" it split in half! Then he took a butter knife and wedged it between the shell and the meat, going all the way around, and out popped the meat. With a sharp knife, he peeled the brown skin off the meat. Follow these same directions in preparing your coconut.

This particular nut did not contain *coconut water.* He told me not to eat one that was dry like this, but only after I had consumed a fourth of it—too late!! Needless to say, I was in no mood to eat anything for a couple of days.

When we see coconuts in the market, they are husked and the outer fibers removed. When checking one out at the store, shake it to see if you can hear the water inside.

When ready to use the coconut, poke openings through two of the "eyes" with an ice pick. The "eye" which is slightly swollen is the easiest one to puncture. Drain out the liquid. This is *coconut water.* You may consume it, but just because it's so good, don't overdo it.

Baking Method: Drain *coconut water.* Place nut in shallow pan. Bake in 300 degree oven about 45 minutes. Remove from oven. This makes the cracking with a hammer very easy. It may even crack while baking.

Coconut Milk: You can buy the milk frozen or make your own. Pour 2 cups boiling water over 4 cups of grated coconut. Let stand 30 minutes. Strain through a double thickness of cheesecloth. Squeeze to remove all liquid. *Coconut milk* may be stored in the refrigerator for several hours before using or frozen for 2 to 3 weeks.

Important note: If you use commercial *coconut milk* that contains additives in recipes, the flavor is just not good. The best substitute is regular milk and coconut extract.

Coconut Cream: A thick creamy substance skimmed off the top of the *coconut milk.* It is found in cans at the market and is good as a sauce, whipped topping, or for various recipes.

Keep in mind the differences in coconut water, milk, and cream and you won't end up with some of the kitchen disasters I have had!

GLOSSARY

Most of these foods or spices can be found in the specialty sections in large grocery markets. Your local Oriental food store is also a good place to shop.

Bamboo Shoots - Edible shoots of certain bamboo plants. Sold in cans. Store leftover shoots in refrigerator, changing water daily. May be stored about two weeks.

Bok Choy - Also called Chinese Cabbage or Celery Cabbage. A loosely packed vegetable with large, dark green leaves and long white stems. Available at most supermarket produce sections.

Chinese Five Spices - Also called Chinese Five Seasons (Ng Heong Fun). An unusual combination of star anise, anise pepper, fennel, cloves and cinnamon. Good substitutes are cloves or allspice.

Chinese Parsley - An herb with long, flat, serrated leaves. Has a stronger taste than regular parsley.

Chutney - A spicy relish made from fruits, herbs and spices.

Cloud Ear Mushrooms - Dried mushrooms found in Oriental markets. When soaked, they expand to 5 times their dried size. Usually used in Asian dishes.

Daikon - Japanese pickled turnip. You may substitute regular turnip but it will change the flavor of the dish.

Ginger Root - A light brown root that provides a clean hot taste and aromatic fragrance. Originally used in Oriental dishes, it has found its way into many recipes in the Islands as well as the Mainland. Found in the produce section. Always peel before using. Slice, mince, or grate for cooking. Ginger root may be placed in an airtight plastic bag and frozen.

Hoisin Sauce - A very flavorful Chinese sauce that is sweet and pungent. It is made from soy beans, sugar, flour, vinegar, salt, garlic, chili and sesame. A good condiment with pork, roast duck, and in marinades for poultry. Keeps indefinitely. Also a good substitute for plum sauce.

Lily Buds - Used in Chinese cooking as a traditional ingredient in Mu Shu Pork. They are dried day lily buds, and must be soaked in warm water 30 minutes, then drained, before using. Available at Oriental grocery stores.

Lomi Lomi Salmon - A dish made of fresh salted salmon, usually served at Luaus and in Hawaiian homes.

Long Rice - Translucent bean threads made from mung bean flour. Must be soaked in water about 30 minutes before cooking to absorb flavor of food with which they are cooked. Cellophane noodles may be substituted.

Lychee - A Chinese fruit, readily available in cans at Oriental food markets. Has a brown skin and a very sweet white meat.

Kona Coffee - A gourmet delight around the world. Grown on the "Big Island" of Hawaii. It has a rare deep rich flavor. Enjoyed as is, but most often it is blended. May be found in gourmet shops.

Macadamia Nuts - Hawaii's elegant macadamia nut is a delicacy sought after by international chefs and creative cooks. They are found in the nut section of the market, usually in glass jars. Expensive, yes, but the demand far exceeds the supply. They also freeze well.

Mango - Comes in all sizes and kinds. Distinctive in flavor and high in fiber content. No substitute. Great in fruit desserts, salads and beverages. They are very sweet and delicious as is. Found in the fresh fruit department.

Oyster Sauce - A spicy concentrate made from liquid in which oysters have been cooked. Keeps indefinitely.

Papaya - Pear shaped fruit with a sweet golden flesh. High in nutritional value.

Passion Fruit or Lilikoi - This is a plum-sized yellow and purple fruit. It got its name, Hawaiian Passion Fruit or Lilikoi, for the district on Maui where the trees were first planted many years ago. It is available as a frozen concentrate on the Mainland and is delightful combined with other fruits and in beverages.

Poi - Steamed Taro root made into a thick paste. Comes fresh or freeze dried. See package for directions.

Pupu - Hawaiian finger foods. Appetizers.

Sake - Japanese rice wine. Colorless and relatively fragrance free until heated.

Sesame Oil - An amber-colored oil made from sesame seeds. Used mainly for flavoring; do not use as a frying oil.

Snow Peas - Also known as Chinese Peas. They have flat, light green pods with a small pea inside. The entire pea is edible. Mostly used in wok or stir-fry dishes. Found in frozen food or fresh produce section of market.

Soy Sauce - Very popular now in the United States. Made from soy beans, barley and salt. It was introduced to Hawaii by the Orientals. Has become a principal part of most Island cookery. Called Shoyu in Hawaii. Very salty.

Tempura - Japanese method of frying. Vegetables and seafood fried in a light colored and lacey batter.

Ti Leaves - Large dark green leaves of the Ti plant. Used for wrappers in Hawaiian cooking; also for a garnish on which to serve food.

Toasted Sesame Seeds - The nut-like flavor of sesame seeds is enhanced when lightly toasted.

Tofu - Tofu is soft white bean curd formed into a block. It has a bland taste, but absorbs the flavor and aroma of the foods with which it is cooked. One of the finest sources of protein. Also low in cholesterol. Usually comes in blocks packed in water. Found in a refrigerated section in the market.

Water Chestnut - A crispy white vegetable. Available canned in most markets.

Won Ton - A crispy dumpling made with a Won Ton Pi (wrapper) filled and deep fried. May be steamed or cooked soft in soup.

Won Ton Pi - A sheet of pasta dough used to make Won Ton. Often fried crisp without fillings and used in salads instead of croutons.

Aloha
Mae and Lee

153

INDEX

Hawaiian Magic

Share the magic of paradise with friends, clients and associates.

Just order and leave the shipping to us.

send order (make checks payable) to:

BESS PRESS, INC.
P.O. Box 22388
Honolulu, Hawaii 96822

**Hawaiian Magic
$9.95 plus $2.00 shipping and handling.**

Quantity _____

Amount per Book _____

Shipping and Handling _____

Total _____

Please Print Clearly

Name _____

Address _____

City _____ State _____ Zip _____

Name of a store in your area who would like to sell this book _____

Another fine book for your collection!

Add 4% sales tax on orders delivered in the state of Hawaii.